ROMAN LAW
IN
MEDIÆVAL
EUROPE

✦

BY

PAUL
VINOGRADOFF

THE LAWBOOK
EXCHANGE, LTD.
Clark, New Jersey

ISBN 978-1-58477-109-8

Lawbook Exchange edition 2001, 2018

The quality of this reprint is equivalent to the quality of the original work.

THE LAWBOOK EXCHANGE, LTD.
33 Terminal Avenue
Clark, New Jersey 07066-1321

*Please see our website for a selection of our other publications
and fine facsimile reprints of classic works of legal history:*
www.lawbookexchange.com

Library of Congress Cataloging-in-Publication Data

Vinogradoff, Paul, Sir, 1854-1925.
    Roman law in mediaeval Europe / by Paul Vinogradoff.
        p. cm.
    Originally published: London ; New York : Harper, 1909.
    Includes bibliographical references.
    ISBN 1-58477-109-7 (cloth: alk. paper)
        1. Roman law. 2. Law--Europe--History. I. Title.

KJA147.V56 2000
340.5'4--dc21   00-039068

Printed in the United States of America on acid-free paper

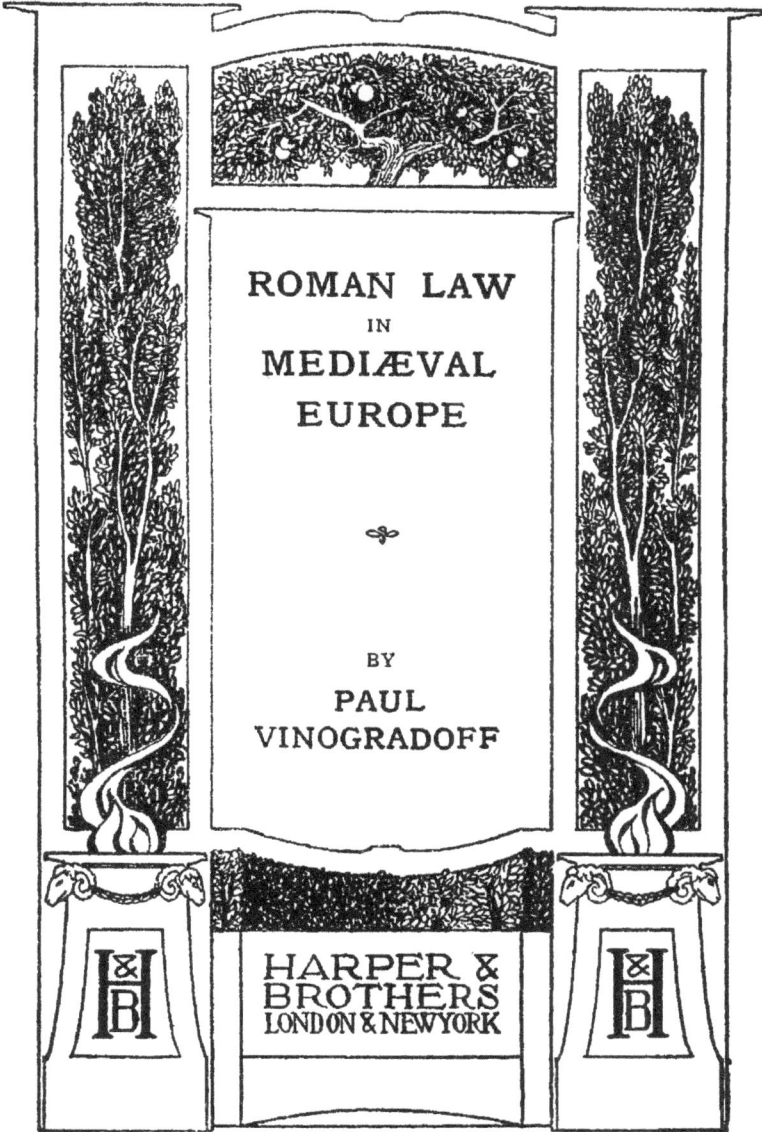

ROMAN LAW
IN
MEDIÆVAL
EUROPE

❦

BY

PAUL
VINOGRADOFF

HARPER &
BROTHERS
LONDON & NEW YORK

ROMAN LAW

IN

MEDIÆVAL EUROPE

BY

PAUL VINOGRADOFF

M.A., D.C.L., LL.D., DR. HIST., F.B.A.

CORPUS PROFESSOR OF JURISPRUDENCE
IN THE UNIVERSITY OF OXFORD
HONORARY PROFESSOR OF HISTORY
IN THE UNIVERSITY OF MOSCOW

LONDON AND NEW YORK
HARPER & BROTHERS
45 ALBEMARLE STREET, W.
1909

PREFACE

THE sketch of a great historical process presented in the following chapters is based on lectures delivered in the spring of 1909 as an advanced historical course on the invitation of the University of London. I have not attempted to trace the history of Roman Law in the Middle Ages in all its details or even in all its stages, but I have tried to characterise the principal epochs of this development in Western Europe. One of the reasons for publishing this essay consists in the fact that there is no English account of the mediæval life of Roman Law similar to the masterly tracts of Modderman and v. Below. I have given references at the foot of the pages very sparingly, and have cited in connection with each lecture only the books which have been used in preparing it. But a few fragments from the texts have been added in an Appendix to illustrate some points as to which it was important to

PREFACE

consider the very words of the original authorities.

I take this occasion to thank the Dean and Chapter of Worcester for the loan of their famous MS. of Vacarius' Liber Pauperum.

P. VINOGRADOFF

OXFORD,
October, 1909

CONTENTS

ROMAN LAW
IN MEDIÆVAL EUROPE

LECTURE I

DECAY OF THE ROMAN LAW

Principal authorities: *Mommsen*, Ostgothische Studien in the Neues Archiv für ältere deutsche Geschichtskunde, XIV, 1889; Notitia dignitatum, ed. *Seeck*, 1876; Codex Theodosianus, ed. *Mommsen et Krüger*, 1905; Lex Romana Visigothorum, ed. *Haenel*, 1838; *Conrat* (*Cohn*), Das Breviarium Alaricianum, 1903; *Conrat* (*Cohn*), Der westgothische Gaius; der westgothische Paulus, Verhandlingen der Kon. Akademie van Wetenschoppen te Amsterdam, N.R. VI, 4; and VIII, 4. Lex Romana Curiensis, ed. *Zeumer*, in the Monumenta Germaniæ Historica, Leges, V; *H. Brunner*, Deutsche Rechtsgeschichte, 1906, I², especially §§ 35 and 52; *Savigny*, Geschichte des römischen Rechts im Mittelalter, I, II; *K. Neumeyer*, Die gemeinrechtliche Entwickelung des internationalen Privat und Strafrechts bis Bartolus, I, 1901; *A. von Halban*, Das römische Recht in den germanischen Volksstaaten, I, II, III, 1899–1907; *J. Ficker*, Untersuchungen zur Erbenfolge der ostgermanischen Rechte, I–V, 1891–1902; Leges Visigothorum. *Zeumer*, in the Monumenta Germaniæ historica, Leges, in 4to; Leges Langobardorum, ed. *Bluhme*, Mon. Germ. hist. Leges, fol. IV; Formulæ regni Francorum, ed. *Zeumer*, in the Mon. Germ. hist., 4to; *H. Brunner*, Zur Rechtsgeschichte der römisch. germanischen Urkunde, 1906; *Fustel de Coulanges*, Histoire des institutions de la France, especially Les origines du Système féodal, 1890;

ROMAN LAW

P. Vinogradoff, Romanistische Einflüsse im Angel-
sächsischen Recht: das Buchland in the Mélanges Fitting,
II, 1908 ; *H. Fitting*, Die juristischen Schriften des
früheren Mittelalters, 1876 ; *M. Conrat*, Geschichte der
Quellen und der Litteratur des römischen Rechts im
früheren Mittelalter, 1891 ; *J. Flach*, Études d'histoire du
droit Romain, 1893 ; Isidori Hispalensis Etymologiæ
sive Origines, in the Corpus grammaticorum latinorum
veterum, ed. *Lindemann*, III, 1833 ; Lex Romana
Canonice Compta, ed. *Conrat*, in the Transactions of the
Amsterdam Academy, 1904.

WITHIN the whole range of history there
is no more momentous and puzzling problem than that connected with the fate of Roman
Law after the downfall of the Roman State.
How is it that a system shaped to meet certain
historical conditions not only survived those
conditions, but has retained its vitality even
to the present day, when political and social
surroundings are entirely altered ? Why is it
still deemed necessary for the beginner in jurisprudence to read manuals compiled for Roman
students who lived more than 1500 years ago ?
How are we to account for the existence of such
hybrid beings as Roman Dutch Law or of the
recently superseded modern Roman Law of
Germany ? How did it come about that the
Germans, instead of working out their legal
system in accordance with national precedents,
and with the requirements of their own country,
broke away from their historical jurisprudence
to submit to the yoke of bygone doctrines of a

foreign empire ? Surely these and kindred questions are well worthy of the attention of lawyers, historians, and students of social science. I cannot attempt to cover the whole ground in the discussion of such a problem, but it may be of some value to sketch the chief lines of the subject in regard to the principal countries of Western Europe during the Middle Ages. It was mainly at that time that there took place the momentous process, not inappropriately called by German scholars 'the Reception of Roman Law.'

We shall have to deal with laws and law books, with doctrine and casuistry—all topics devoid of romantic charm. But there is a peculiar interest, as I conceive it, in watching the play of social forces and human conceptions. I should like here to recall the words of one of the masters of modern historical study : " The history of Institutions cannot be mastered—can scarcely be appreciated—without an effort. It affords little of the Romantic interest or of the picturesque grouping which constitute the charm of history in general, and holds but small temptation to the mind that requires to be tempted to study the truth. But it has a deep value and an abiding interest to those who have the courage to work upon it." *

We may call this interest a scientific one,

* Stubbs, *Constitutional History*, Introduction.

because, although the methods of social science and of natural science are necessarily different, their aims are identical. Both strive to ascertain the causes of events in order to pave the way for the formulation of laws of development.

1. The story I am about to tell is, in a sense, a ghost story. It treats of a second life of Roman Law after the demise of the body in which it first saw the light. I must assume a general acquaintance with the circumstances in which that wonderful doctrinal system arose and grew. My tale begins at the epoch of decay during which the Western Empire was engaged in its last struggles with overwhelming hordes of barbarians. It was the time when the new languages and nations of Western Europe were born ; when the races gathered within the boundaries fixed by Augustus, Trajan, and Septimius Severus were permeated by Latin culture ; when the elements of Romance and Teutonic Europe were gradually beginning to assume some shape. The period may be studied from two opposite points of view : it was characterised by the Romanisation of the provinces and by the barbarisation of Rome. As it is forcibly put by Lampridius in his Biography of Alexander Severus, the Roman world was crowded with undesirable aliens. No wonder that the standard of culture rapidly fell while the range of Roman influence was extended. We seem to watch a great stream

emerging into the expanse of a delta ; its waters become shallow, sluggish, and discoloured by the quantities of sand it carries with it. The gradual transformation of racial elements is especially manifest in military organisation. Sturdy Illyrians, Thracians, Goths, and Franks were substituted for the national legions of Italy or Gaul, and it was only through the influx of these recruits that the emperors of the fourth and fifth centuries were able to stave off temporarily the threatening catastrophe. The transformation of the army went so far that the expression ' barbarian ' (*barbarus*) came to be commonly used in the sense of soldier. As pagan became an equivalent of heathen, instead of indicating the country folk, so barbarian was used in the sense of military man. Nor were the foreign soldiers merely individual recruits. They were settled in whole troops in the provinces, and their settlements were organised as separate administrative districts. The official Calendar of the Empire, the *Notitia Dignitatum*, mentions *læti* in Gaul ; we hear of Sarmatians and Suevi as *Gentiles* in Italy. Whole nations, such as the Burgundians, the Visigoths, the Ostgoths, the Franks, were admitted as allies (*fœderati*) within the limits of the Empire, and quartered in the provinces in a way that made them practically masters of a third, sometimes even of two-thirds, of the land. This influx of alien immigrants in the provinces of the West was bound to make itself felt in the legal domain. The Empire was forced to recognise to some extent the legal customs of the various tribes, and the idea of wiping out these customs in favour of the civilised law of Rome was never entertained. As evidence of this invasion of barbarian customs, we may quote the words of Bishop Theoderetos (middle of the fifth century). After having spoken of the unity of government and law achieved by the Empire, he qualifies the statement by the remark that the Ethiopians, Caucasian tribes, and barbarians in general were left to follow their own legal customs with regard to transactions among themselves. This raises a question which came to be of vital importance somewhat later, namely, how were members of different tribes to transact business when they met ? The supreme authority of the Imperial Courts and of Roman Law did not allow these divergences to assume a sharp and uncompromising aspect, but as alien customs were allowed within its boundaries, the principle that a man must be made answerable primarily to his own personal law existed already in germ in the closing centuries of the Western Empire.

2. A second result of great moment was the fact that Roman Law, even so far as it was recognised and practised by the barbarians in the provinces, began to take the shape of a body

of debased rules. Though many of the characteristic institutions of Roman legal antiquity were
still in vigour, they had ceased to represent a
high level of juridical culture. Three principal
statements of barbarised Roman Law arose at
the close of the fifth and at the beginning of
the sixth century : the Edicts of the Ostgothic
kings, the Lex Romana Burgundionum, and
the Roman Law of the Visigoths (Breviarium
Alaricianum) compiled in 506 by order of King
Alaric II. Of these three, the latter exerted the
greatest influence. While the Edicts of the
Ostgothic kings lost their significance after the
destruction of their kingdom by the Byzantines,
while the law of the Romans in Burgundy remained local, the Visigothic compilation became
the standard source of Roman Law throughout
Western Europe during the first half of the Middle
Ages. The Breviarium Alaricianum purposed
to be, and indeed was, a more or less complete
Code for the usage of the Roman populations of
France and Spain. And it deserves attention
as evidence of the state to which Roman Law
had been reduced by the beginning of the sixth
century.

It still testifies to considerable knowledge
and experience. Its Latin is sufficiently pure ;
it presents a reasoned attempt to compress the
enactments of the later Empire into a compendium
of moderate size. The texts are accompanied

by an interpretation composed either just before
Alaric's code, or in connection with it, and intended to make the sense of the laws as simple
and clear as possible. It is not to be wondered
that the Breviarium obtained a dominant position
in European Western countries. The Corpus Juris
of Justinian, which contains the main body of
Roman Law for later ages, including our own,
was accepted and even known only in the East
and in those parts of Italy which had been re-
conquered by Justinian's generals. The rest
of the Western provinces still clung to the tradition of the preceding period culminating in
the official Code of Theodosius II (A.D. 437).
In the fifth century, lawyers had to take account
of the legislative acts of Constantine and his
successors up to 437, of fragments of earlier
legislation gathered together in the private com-
pilations of Gregorius and Hermogenes, of the
" Novellæ " of fifth-century emperors, and of
a vast unwieldy body of jurisprudence as laid
down in legal opinions and treatises of the first
three centuries A.D. Even after the achievement of the commissioners of Theodosius, the
despairing remarks of Theodosius II on the state
of the law in his time remained to a great extent
true. One of the principal reasons of the "pallid
hue of night studies of Roman Law," as he
expresses it, was undoubtedly connected with
the "immense quantity of learned treatises; the

variety of actionable remedies, the difficulties of case law, and the huge bulk of imperial enactments which raised up a dense wall of fog against all attempts of the human mind to master it." It was a rather fine performance of the "barbarian" Visigothic king to attempt, in 506, with the help of his nobles, his clergy, and the representatives of provinces, to do for the Roman population under his sway what Justinian did some thirty years later with infinitely greater resources at his disposal for the Eastern Empire.

3. The comparison with Justinian's Code is also instructive in other respects. Both Codes fall into the same three fundamental subdivisions— that of the Institutes, of Common Law (*jus*), and of the Statutes (*leges*). The first consists of an introductory survey for beginners, the second of jurisprudential doctrines as laid down by legal authorities, and the third of the enactments of recent emperors. Each division is represented in the Breviarium. As a parallel to Justinian's Institutes, the Breviarium introduces an abstract from Gaius. The choice of this authority was very appropriate, but it was necessary to revise Gaius. And in the hands of Alaric's commissioners the introductory treatise served a purely utilitarian, not a scholarly, purpose. Accordingly, we find eliminated from the text all antiquarian notices such, for instance, as the distinctions between various kinds of free-born

citizens, the Quirites, the Latini, the dediticii,
although corresponding distinctions were maintained as regards freedmen. Controversial matter
was also omitted, and the text revised with a
view to greater simplicity and clearness. Some
important parts of the Institutes were surrendered
in the course of this process of simplification;
for example, the teaching on sources of law, on
the contrasting systems of the *jus civile* and the
jus gentium, and the whole of Gaius' treatment
of actions. In all these respects the Visigothic
version of Gaius presents a complete contrast
with the handling of Gaius' text in the schools
of grammar of the fifth-century Empire, as exemplified by the Autun MS. of Gaius.

This shrinking of the intellectual horizon is
even more striking in the second subdivision,
the part devoted to *jus*—the legal doctrine and
jurisprudence of common law, as we should term
it nowadays. It consists, in Justinian's Corpus,
of the stupendous collection of extracts from
the great jurists of the first, second, and third
centuries, known as the Digest. The barbarians
were even more unfit to bear the weight of such
a "mass of wisdom" (*ad portandum tantæ sap-
ientiæ molem*) than the Roman citizens of the sixth
century. The corresponding element in the
Breviarium is represented mainly by an abstract
from the sentences of one of the great third-
century jurists—Paul, and by a stray text from

Papinian. The sentences of Paul were treated from the same point of view of practical usefulness as the Institutes of Gaius, although, as we are not in possession of a complete edition of the original work, we are unable to judge so well of the amount of text omitted by the Visigothic editors. Still, the general directions of the changes in the text can be ascertained, and these leave no doubt that discussions of too learned a character as well as antiquarian notices were excluded. Thus the output of the older jurisconsults, Labeo, Scævola, Sabinus, and their compeers, and nearly the whole of the admirable doctrinal work of Papinian, Ulpian, Modestinus, Gaius, and Paul, with the exception of the educational manuals of the two latter, went overboard at the time of the Visigothic codification, as too learned and too complicated for the age. This renouncement of the best inheritance of Roman Law by men who were themselves neither ignorant nor incompetent, speaks volumes for the great decline in the level of culture, and is especially remarkable in the provinces of Spain and Gaul, where there still existed a compact Roman population.

A similar decay may be observed in the third part of the Breviarium, the part devoted to the *leges*, i.e. the enactments of emperors. The Breviarium makes its selection from a practical point of view. Omissions are again more characteristic than changes. The substitutions of

Curia for the provincial governor and of municipal justices (*judices civitatum*) for the prætor are not especially noteworthy. But, although all the sixteen books of the Theodosianus appear in some form or other in the Breviarium, it is important to notice that the sixth, for example, treating of civil officers and their attributions, is represented by two enactments instead of thirty-eight, and the next one, the seventh, bearing on military organisation, by one law instead of twenty-seven. Such shrinkage is noticeable throughout ; in this case it arises not so much from a change of intellectual culture as from a difference in administrative arrangements and the decay of governmental institutions.

4. The Breviarium Alaricianum consists of laws and rules that are in any case reasonable and tolerably well expressed. A later document of legal tradition, the *Lex Romana Curiensis*, of the end of the eighth century, testifies to a further and deeper decay. This is a statement of legal custom, drawn up for the Romance population of Eastern Switzerland, and used in the Tyrol and Northern Italy as well. Its language and contents are most barbarous. Though the influence of Rome is manifest in the borrowing of legal institutions, the juridical treatment is in no way better, and often worse, than that of contemporary Frankish or Lombard legal customs.

The law in question is based on a very imperfect

abstract of the Lex Romana Visigothorum, in which the Institutes of Gaius and the greater part of Paul's Sententiæ are dropped, while the enactments of emperors are generally taken from the text of the "Interpretation." To what extent some of these enactments were misunderstood by the Grisons ecclesiastics and judges, may be gathered from one or two examples. The latter actually had the courage to quote the "Novella" of Valentinian III on the use of the works of ancient jurisconsults.* There is not much harm in the fact that Gaius appears in their text as Gaggius and Scævola as Scifola. But the emperor's direction that if opinions conflict, authorities should be counted, and a casting vote allowed to Papinian as the greatest, is interpreted by the Rætians to mean that every party to a suit ought to produce witnesses and oath-helpers, and if the number of these prove equal, the case must be decided in favour of the side whose contention is countenanced by Papianus. Even apart from the fact that Papianus is a corruption of Papinianus, originating in the Lex Romana Burgundionum, this reference to a legal authority, which was not even in use in the region in question, completes the muddle. And it is clear that the paragraph as it stands neither corresponds to the original nor could be put into practice.

* See App. I.

There are many scattered traces of barbaric usage making its way into the debased Roman Law of the Rætian country. *Fredum*, the price for peace obtained through the intervention of public authorities, appears here under the same conditions as in Frankish districts. The *Dos*, the possession of which was guaranteed to the wife of a criminal whose property had been confiscated, is the German dower, settled on the wife by the husband, not the Roman dos, brought by the wife to the common household. One of the enactments of the Theodosian Code and of Alaric's Breviarium on lawful marriage, emphasising the importance of the consent of both bride and bridegroom, is stated in such a way that it is possible to catch a glimpse of a wedding ceremony performed before a *judex*, a ruler of some kind, and an assembly of neighbours (VII, 3). It is evident that we are in the presence of a rather debased and Germanised form of legal custom, engrafted on fragments of what had been once a system of Imperial law.

5. We must next inquire in what way, and how far, the degenerated legal customs of Rome were applied in the early Middle Ages. It must be noticed firstly, that no State of this period was strong enough to enforce a compact legal order of its own, excluding all other laws, or treating them as enactments confined to aliens. Even the most powerful of the barbarian governments

raised on the ruins of the Empire, such as the Lombard or Frankish, dealt with a state of affairs based on a mixture of legal arrangements. The Carolingian rulers and especially Charlemagne, introduced some unity in matters of vital importance to the government or to public safety, but, even in their time, racial differences were allowed to crop up everywhere. Law became necessarily personal and local in its application. Both facts must be considered in connection with the survival of Roman legal rules.

The forcible entry of the Goths, Lombards, and Franks into the provinces did not in any sense involve the disappearance or denationalisation of the Roman inhabitants. The legal status of the latter was allowed to continue. The personality of a Roman was valued in a peculiar way, differing from the barbarians that surrounded him. If it cost 200 solidi to atone for the homicide of a Frank, it cost 100 solidi to kill a Roman in Frankish Gaul. All intercourse between Romans was ruled by the law of their race. When a Roman of Toulouse married a girl of the same race, she brought him a *dos* in accordance with Paul's Sententiæ, II, 22, 1 ; he exercised a father's authority over his children, on the strength of the ancient custom of *patria potestas*, as modified by the laws of Constantine. If a landowner wanted to sell his property, he would do it of his own free will, according to the rules of *emptio venditio*. If he wished to dispose of his property after his decease, he would be able to draw up a will making provision for bequests to be paid out by his heir, but carefully avoiding to bequeath more than three-fourths of his property, in conformity with the Lex Falcidia. In all these and in many other respects the legal rights of the Roman would be at variance with those of his German neighbours. These, again would act differently, each according to his peculiar nationality, as Salian Franks or Ripuarians, Bavarians or Burgundians, etc. The position became very intricate when members of different nationalities, living under different laws, were brought together to transact business with each other. As Bishop Agobard of Lyons tells us about 850, it happened constantly that of five people meeting in one room, each followed a law of his own. We find, in fact, in these cross-relationships very striking examples of so-called conflicts of law. Before proceeding to examine the material questions at issue, it was necessary for the judges to discover to what particular body or bodies of law the case belonged. The report of a trial between the monasteries of Fleury on the Loire and St. Denis provides a good illustration of the points raised on such occasions. The case was brought before the tribunal of the Frankish Court. It was found necessary to adjourn it, because both plaintiff and defendant were ecclesiastical corporations, and as such, entitled to a judgment according to Roman Law, of which none of the judges was cognisant. Experts in Roman Law are summoned as assessors, and the trial proceeds at the second meeting of the tribunal. The parties would like to prove their right by single combat between their witnesses, but one of the assessors of the court protests against the waging of battle, on the ground that such a mode of proof would be contrary to Roman Law. The point at issue is therefore examined and decided according to Roman rules of procedure, that is, by production of witnesses and documents. St. Bennet, however, the patron of the Abbey of Fleury, was seemingly prejudiced in favour of the Frankish mode of proof-by-battle, as he revenged himself on the too forward assessor by striking him dumb.*

The rules as to allowing or disallowing recourse to one or the other personal law were necessarily rather complicated. For instance, the payment of fines for crimes was apportioned according to the law of the criminal, and not of the offended person. As regards contracts, each party was held bound by the rule of its own law; but if the contract was accompanied by a wager, it was interpreted according to the law of the

* Miracula S. Benedicti; Mon. Germ., XV[1], p. 490, quoted by Brunner, I[2], p. 394. '

party making the wager. In the case of a contract corroborated by a deed (*carta*), the legal
form and interpretation depended on the status
of the person executing the deed. Some cases
were rendered more complex by the fact that
the courts found it necessary to consider not only
the legal status of the grantor, but also the quality
of the disposable property. For example, in an
Italian charter of 780, we find that a certain
Felix makes a donation to his daughter, and
receives from her a *launegild*, a compensation,
according to Lombard Law, although, as a clerk,
he is himself subject to Roman Law. The reason
is that, while still a layman, he received the property in question from his wife according to
Lombard Law.

6. The confusion resulting from such cross-
relations of personal legal status was not lessened
by the fact that in almost every jurisdictional district, local customs arose to regulate the ordinary
dealings of its population. In districts with a
clearly preponderating racial majority these customs assumed a specific national colouring—
Lombard, Frankish, Roman, as the case might
be. Local customs become in course of time a
very marked characteristic of the Middle Ages.
They tend to restrict the application of the purely
personal principle, although the latter was not
entirely abolished for a long time. The way in
which the light of Roman legal lore was trans-

formed while breaking through the many-coloured panes of local custom was most varied. It is sufficient for our present purpose to note the geographical boundaries of the regions where legal customs were built up on the basis of Roman Law. The area was a wide one. It covered, firstly, Southern Italy, where the Byzantine Empire upheld its authority, until the advent of the Saracens and of the Normans. Here the courts administered not only Roman Law as laid down in the *Corpus Juris*, but also the legislation of Justinian's successors. In the centre, the district forming the so-called Romagna was characterised by the application of Justinian's Code. Thirdly, in Southern France and Northern Spain, the Breviarium Alaricianum reigned supreme.

Now, by laying stress on these geographical limits, I do not mean that Roman legal customs did not assert themselves outside the mentioned regions. On the contrary, throughout the proper domain of barbaric laws, in Northern France, in Germany, and even in England, the influence of certain Roman institutions was manifest in many ways. Even where there was no numerous Roman population to represent the Roman racial element, the clergy, at least, followed Roman Law, and many rules of the latter were adopted for their practical utility.

Let us notice some of these borrowings of the barbarians during the early Middle Ages.

ROMAN LAW

Roman influence was strongest in the case of the Goths. They had been in contact with the Empire at the time of its comparative strength— in the third and fourth centuries. Their two chief branches were settled for a considerable time on Imperial soil as confederates, very un- ruly and dangerous confederates indeed, as Rome came to feel at the hands of Alaric I, but still as confederates who learned constantly from their civilised neighbours. In consequence of this long permeation of Roman customs and legal ideas, we find firstly, that the Ostgoths founded their legislation directly on Roman patterns, and secondly that the Visigoths of Spain and France adopted Roman enactments wholesale, apart from the fact that, as we have seen, they codified Imperial law for the use of their Roman fellow-citizens. Already in the fragments of the laws of Euric, the most ancient part of Visi- gothic legislation (about 464), we find a number of paragraphs drawn from Roman sources, for example, the clause forbidding actions con- cerning events which had occurred more than thirty years previously (*c.* 277) ; the declaration, that donations extorted by force or intimidation (*vi aut metu*) are to be null and void (*c.* 309), a rule which breaks through the purely formalistic treatment of obligations natural to barbaric law ; the admission of equality between men and women as to inheritance (*c.* 320), etc. Later on, during the sixth century, the influence of Roman rules becomes stronger and stronger. Entire sections are adopted by the Lex Visigothorum, from the Breviarium, the Novellæ, and from customary laws of Roman origin which still lingered in the courts, in spite of the official codification of Alaric II. About one-third of the so-called *antiqua* goes back to Roman sources. As to the legislation of the great kings of the seventh century, Chindaswind and Recceswind, who made an attempt to replace personal laws by territorial codes, the greater part of it is based on Roman patterns. It must, however, be said of this overwhelming Romanisation that it is to some extent exaggerated in official laws. Ficker's remarkable investigations have shown that there was a continuous stream of Germanic legal customs running counter to the Romanising tendencies of royal enactments, and maintaining rules and institutions which remind us strongly of Scandinavian custom, and evidently go back to a Teutonic origin. These Germanic elements emerge again in the later statements of provincial customs, the so-called Fueros. But, even if we allow for the existence of such an undercurrent of Germanic custom, the general inference is not destroyed that Roman legal lore had a most powerful influence on the Visigoths of Spain and France.

The history of the Lombards discloses a different

state of affairs. The very large Roman population of Northern and Central Italy was neither destroyed nor entirely bereft of its legal inheritance. But the practice of its law was confined to voluntary transactions and to forms of arbitration, resembling those which were in use among Christians before the Church was recognised by the Empire. It is known that votaries of the Christian faith tried to avoid interference from heathen magistrates by settling their disputes through arbitration. Something of the same kind preserved the tradition of Roman Law in Lombard districts in the course of the sixth and seventh centuries, until it was laid down expressly by an enactment of Liutprand (cl. 91) that instruments made before Roman notaries should conform to the rules of Roman Law in the same way as Lombard deeds should be drawn up according to Lombard Law. Although the existence of a body of Roman Law was indirectly recognised in this fashion, no provision was made, even after the above enactment, for the creation of Roman tribunals or the appointment of judges versed in this particular law. We are left to surmise that when cases necessitating the application of Roman rules came before the Lombard courts, the Germanic judges obtained help from assessors acquainted with Roman Law, and probably chosen from among those very notaries mentioned in Liutprand's enactment.

DECAY OF THE ROMAN LAW

Now it is remarkable that although Lombard legislation thus remains true to its Teutonic origin as regards the contents of legal rules, it nevertheless lay open to the powerful influence of Roman Law from two different sides. Firstly, the rapid growth of economic intercourse in Italy with its complicated relations, requiring nice adjustment, rendered a recourse to civilised law highly desirable, more especially as many parties to business affairs were people of Roman birth, and as transactions with citizens of the Exarchate and of Southern Italy living directly under Roman rule were of every day occurrence. This particular means of permeation is represented by the growth of Lombardic *formulæ* for the framing of contracts, which are evidently influenced by Roman patterns. A second path was laid open to the invasion of Roman ideas by the appearance of juridical reflection. In the legislation of the purely Lombard epoch at the beginning of the eighth century, we find already traces of jurisprudential analysis. There is, for instance, an enactment of Liutprand (*c.* 134),* treating of the ejectment of a landed proprietor by his neighbours. If, in the course of these violent proceedings, he suffers bodily harm, the offenders must, of course, pay the fine for the homicide or wounding, but the legislator declares in addition that they are guilty

* See App. II.

of conspiracy, and must be fined 20 solidi on that account. In analysing the case, Liutprand, or his legal advisers, explain why they decree such a fine and not another. They state their reasons for ¬not considering the transgression to be one of ' *arischild*,' that is, of forming an armed band (cf. Roth. 19, Liutpr. 35, 141), not a case of unlawful organisation of country folk (*consilium rusticanorum*, Roth. 279), nor of riot (*rusticanorum seditio*). It seems to the legislator that the material point in the case lies in the preparation to commit murderous assault. It is this intention which constitutes the criminal element in the conspiracy, and which may lead to the perpetration of the crime. In spite of the barbarous language, the mode of reasoning testifies to a rising level of juridical thought; and, though a direct connection with Roman rules is not traceable, yet this and similar cases of legal analysis in Lombard legislation, suggest that Lombard justice was progressing from a naive application of barbarian rules to a reflective jurisprudence, and this undoubtedly opened the way for a consideration of Roman doctrine.

In the Frankish Empire we have before us a third example of the process of permeation of barbaric law by Roman notions. The resistance to foreign law is stronger in this case than even in that of the Lombards. The Salic and Ripuarian Codes are based almost exclusively on Teutonic principles. And yet there were many channels by which Roman legal ideas assert themselves. Firstly, there is the influence of the Church, which has left its mark more especially on Bavarian law and on the capitularies of the kings and emperors of Carolingian race. Secondly, there is the influence of Roman rules on private transactions. In this field the barbarians left a wide margin for the settlement of legal difficulties by private agreements between parties, provided such agreements did not infringe some established or formulated rule of law. Large gaps in the barbaric enactments concerning the settlement of business matters had to be filled up, and this was achieved by extensive borrowing from Roman legal materials. Abundant evidence is afforded in this respect by the Frankish collections of *formulæ*, that is, ready-made models of legal instruments. Such ancient collections as those of Marculf, of Anjou, of Tours, are full of instruments framed on the pattern of Roman deeds ; and a history of barbaric legal instruments must start in every case from beginnings laid down by Roman precedents. To mention just one or two cases : a formula of Marculf shows clearly the breach made into Germanic customs of succession by the theory of the equality of sexes in regard to inheritance admitted by Roman Law : a father bequeaths land to his daughter, in spite of the Salic Law reserving land to the male sex (II, 10). The emancipation from slavery is mostly carried out according to Roman rules constituting a relation of client-ship between the freedman and his former master or to the Church, etc.

Even England, the country least affected by Roman influence, does not form an exception in this respect. The Old English Books, which constitute grants of private property exempted from the application of Folkright, are, to a great extent, a Romanesque importation effected by the Church in conjunction with the kings. Their chief aim was to substitute a form of property similar to that known to Roman Law, for the landownership restricted by tribal custom, which represented the barbaric mode of land tenure in England.

7. The life of Roman Law in the barbaric states, as far as we have considered it hitherto, was upheld by the continuance of fragmentary and garbled rules derived more or less directly from the system formed during the prosperous periods of Roman civilisation. Can it be said that the barbaric successors of Papinian and Ulpian, of Marcus Aurelius and Constantine, kept also up, to some extent, the threads of theoretical reflection and intelligent teaching, which in former days had served to combine separate details into a reasoned whole ? Is there a distinct stream of *jurisprudence* winding its

way through the dark ages from the fifth century, when western jurists took part in the codification and interpretation of Imperial Law, to the twelfth century when a body of learned doctrine sprang up again in Italy and France ? These problems have given rise to much controversy among modern scholars. We find such names as those of Stintzing, Fitting, Chiapelli, on one side, and those of Conrat and Flach on the other. It is necessary to take up a position in regard to this discussion, even though there can be no talk of any detailed examination of the arguments adduced on both sides.

To begin with, it seems clear that even legal learning, as distinguished from legal practice, did not entirely disappear with the downfall of the Empire. It survived to some extent together with other remnants of ancient culture, more especially through the agency of the learned classes of those days—-the clerical and monastic orders. The survivals in question, however, are not only slight and incoherent, but, as a rule, hopelessly mixed up with the attempt of the early Middle Ages to effect a kind of salvage of the general learning of antiquity. There are no definite traces of organised schools of law. What legal learning there is remains connected with exercises in grammar, rhetoric, and dialectics. A striking example of the kind of work carried on in the course of the seventh and eighth centuries is presented by the Etymologies or Origins of the Spanish Bishop, Isidor of Seville. It is an *Encyclopædia* embracing all sorts of information collected from classical sources—on arts, medicine, Old and New Testament topics, ecclesiastical history, philology, and law. The legal sections comprise, firstly, generalisations on subdivisions of jurisprudence, on the aims and methods of law, on legislators and jurisconsults ; and, secondly, notices as to substantive law—on witnesses, on deeds, on the law of things, on crime and punishment, etc. All these matters are treated by excerpts from classical literature, from writings of jurisconsults, and from legal enactments. As is shown by the title, the author lays great stress on supposed etymologies for the explanation of institutions and rules. It is needless to say that the philological derivations compiled by him are sometimes fanciful in the extreme. In dealing with legal instruments, for example,* Isidor explains that *donatio* is the same as *doni actio* (the action of a gift), while *dos* (the marriage portion of the bride) comes from *do item* (I give likewise). And this quibble is referred to the fact that in effecting a marriage settlement the gift (of the bridegroom) comes first, while the portion of the bride follows second. In a similar way condition is derived from *condictio* (joint declaration), because the testimony of

* See App. III.

not less than two witnesses can be accepted as evidence (V, 24, 25). There are also many direct misunderstandings, as, for example, when he declares that edicts are enactments of kings or emperors, that *peculium* belongs to minors only, etc. It is characteristic of the state of legal knowledge in the early Middle Ages that these fragments were greatly appreciated and constantly copied and excerpted.

The study of legal books was mainly limited to two narrow grooves. The leisure of clerical life was employed in this particular, as in other fields, in making abstracts from the voluminous productions of the Roman age, and in trying laboriously to discover the literal meaning of expressions. The abstract (Epitome) and the Gloss are the two channels for the tradition of learning in the course of this barren epoch. To illustrate the results achieved by abstracts, one may refer, for example, to the so-called *Lex Romana Canonice compta*, a compilation of Roman laws dating from the ninth century, in which the selection of materials was primarily affected by the wish to provide members of the Church with rules of Roman Laws that might be of use to them.

The work of supplying glosses goes on uninterruptedly from classical times right through the Middle Ages. They were the mediæval substitutes for translations and commentaries. Short renderings, etymologies and explanations were

inserted over the line to facilitate the interpretation of single terms or words, while longer
summaries and notices were jotted down on the
margin. The gloss to a Turin MS. of the Institutes
and the gloss to the Epitome of the Codex in
a MS. belonging to the Dean and Chapter of
Pistoia (Tuscany), may serve as examples of
this type of work. The first was compiled some
time before the tenth century, and was based on
translations of Byzantine notes to all parts of
the *Corpus Juris.* The Pistoia gloss is more
original. Its principal elements date also from
the ninth century, but it was in use all through
the tenth, eleventh, and twelfth centuries, and
grew considerably by later additions. Most of
the notes have been provided by a person of by
no means contemptible intelligence. Though
his direct borrowings from the *Corpus Juris*
cannot always be traced, he shows in his summaries and in his explanatory remarks an understanding of juridical questions, and is quite able
to give the gist of a rule in his own words. For
instance, the Epitome II, 12, 10, gives the words
of an enactment to the effect that, if the representative of a person (procurator) had full powers to
act in the latter's behalf, a decision given against
him in a trial ought to stand; for, in the case
of a fraud, the procurator might be sued by his
principal (Si quid fraudi vel doli egit, conveniri
eum more judiciorum non prohiberis). The gloss

notes shortly : " He who has full power to act can carry a matter to a conclusion unless he commits a fraud " (nota qui habet plenam potesttatem agendi posse rem sine dolo firmiter finire). The idea is the same as in the original, but is formulated from a different point of view. On the strength of these and similar observations we are able to maintain that there was a constant, though thin, stream of legal learning running through the darkest centuries of the Middle Ages, that is, from the fifth to the tenth. The existence of organised law schools is not proved, nor can there be any talk of a very active development of individual thought. But transcripts and abstracts from the fragmentary materials bequeathed by antiquity were made and studied in the scriptoria of monasteries or chapters and in the classrooms of teachers of Arts.

LECTURE II

THE REVIVAL OF JURISPRUDENCE

Authorities : *Savigny*, Geschichte des römischen Rechts im Mittelalter, II,III,IV; *J.Ficker*, Forschungen zur Reichs und Rechtsgeschichte Italiens, 1868–74 ; *N. Tammassia*, Lanfranc arcivescovo di Canterbury e la Scuola Pavese in the Mélanges Fitting, II ; *H. Fitting*, Die Anfänge der Rechtsschule zu Bologna, 1888 ; *Chiappelli*, Lo Studio bolognese, 1888 ; *Modderman*, Die Reception des römischen Rechts, übersetzt von *K. Schurz*, 1875 ; Quæstiones de juris subtilitatibus des Irnerius, ed. by *H. Fitting*, 1894 ; Summa Codicis des Irnerius, ed. by *H. Fitting*, 1894 ; *Besta*, L'opera di Irnerio, 1896 ; *P. Krüger*, Geschichte der Quellen und Litteratur des römischen Rechts, 1888 ; Tourtoulon, Placentin, 1896 ; Dissensiones dominorum, ed. *Haenel*, 1834 ; *E. Landsberg*, Die Glosse des Accursius und ihre Lehre vom Eigenthum, 1883 ; *T. E. Holland*, Vacarius, in the Dictionary of National Biography ; *F. Liebermann*, Magister Vacarius in the English Historical Review, 1896 ; *F. W. Maitland*, Vacarius' Summa de matrimonio, Law Qu. R., 1897 ; *K. Wenck*, Magister Vacarius, 1820 ; *Stölzel*, Ueber Vacarius, in the Zeitschrift für Rechtsgeschichte, VI (1867) ; *Rivalta*, Il rinovamento della giurisprudenza filosofica secondo la Scolastica, 1888 ; *Rivalta*, Dispute celebri del diritto Civile, 1895 ; *Ed. Meynial*, Encore Irnerius in the Nouvelle Revue de droit français et étranger, 1896 ; *S. Brie*, Die Lehre vom Gewohnheitsreche, I, 1899.

1. THE aspect of legal studies begins to change in a remarkable manner about the eleventh century. This epoch witnessed several new departures in the history of Euro-

pean civilisation. The papacy achieved a decisive concentration of power during the pontificate of Gregory VII. Feudalism becomes crystallised into a complete and consistent system. The Norman states arise with the promise of efficient administration and political order. The foundations of Scholasticism are firmly laid in the age of Anselm. The commonwealths of Lombardy begin to earn the fruits of a brilliant economic and cultural progress. It is on this background of returning prosperity and growing self-reliance that we notice a spontaneous awakening of jurisprudence—of theory and learning in the field of law, and this awakening is not confined to one locality. At least four powerful centres of legal learning must be taken into account—one in Provence, still a dependency of the Empire at that time ; the second in the cities of Lombardy ; a third at Ravenna, with its ancient Imperial traditions ; and last, but not least, the famous school of Bologna, the city at the crossways between the Romagna, Lombardy, and Tuscany.

The most striking evidence of the awakening of jurisprudence in Southern France is afforded by a tract on Roman Law, called *Exceptiones Petri*, "Excerpts by Peter," composed some time in the latter half of the eleventh century and dedicated by the unknown author to Odilo, a ' vicarius ' (*viguier*) of Valence in Dauphiné.

The opening passages of its prologue explain the scope of the work. "As it is not possible, even for scholars most learned in the knowledge of laws (etiam juris sapientissimis doctoribus) to come to a definite conclusion in regard to many and different kinds of cases on account of the large number of various scruples, let us unravel the results of juridical decisions and controversies by examining the reason of natural and civil law. If anything in the law be disused, abolished, or contrary to equity (inutile ruptum æquitative contrarium), let us tread it under foot (pedibus concalcamus). Let us reveal to you, Odilo, magnificent master of the most splendid city of Valence, whatever has been discovered anew or tenaciously preserved. So that in the examination of your tribunal and in the terms of your acts there should not appear anything unjust or subject to provocation. But, that all corruption being removed, everything should be resplendent for the sake of the power of justice, of the glory of your dignity, and of the praise of supreme majesty."

You will notice that this introduction, though couched in sounding language, is by no means a flight of empty rhetoric. Every word in it has a definite meaning, and its particulars are worthy of attention. The work of the "Exceptiones" has been prompted by practical considerations, by difficulties experienced, in the administration of the law. It is not merely dedicated to a magistrate of high standing, but is intended to give him help in the exercise of his office. His jurisdiction forms a link in a system culminating in an appeal to "supreme majesty," evidently, in this case, the supreme majesty of the Emperor. The necessity of having recourse to a juridical manual is derived from frequent controversies and doubts among experts in law. The tract uses the expression, *sapientissimis legibus doctoribus,* which, though it cannot be taken in the usual academic sense of doctors of laws, yet is full of meaning, even in the narrower sense used in our translation. It implies a preceding period of study and discussion which would range into the earlier years of the eleventh century. This observation is well in keeping with the contents of the "Exceptiones," which, for all their brevity and occasional misunderstandings, exhibit a remarkably ripe juridical judgment, as well as a considerable acquaintance with the sources of Roman Law.

The author claims great power and responsibility with characteristic self-reliance. He does not scruple to "tread under foot" enactments, which, according to his view, have fallen into disuse, or are contrary to equity, and his only authority for such an act is that of a jurisconsult, of a learned exponent of legal doctrine.

The execution of the work is not unworthy of the design. The "Exceptiones" form a short manual of rules for practical use. Their materials are drawn from the *Corpus Juris*, and not from the *Breviarium Alaricianum*. As the Provençal surroundings of the author cannot be called in question, we must infer that there was in the eleventh century, in the south of France, a marked revival in the study and application of the Law of Justinian, probably in close connection with Italy. All these parts of Justinian's codification have been employed, but it must be noticed that the Novellæ are referred to through the medium of the so-called Julian's Epitome, made about the middle of the sixth century. As for the Digest, it is the so-called "Digestum vetus" (the first twenty-four books) which has been chiefly used, whereas the New Digest (books 39–50) has been utilised much less frequently, and the middle portion (the Infortiatum) has hardly been touched. The practical bent of the author prevents him from ignoring the existence of barbaric laws. He sometimes mentions customs based on Lombard and Frankish enactments, as, for example, when he states that a fine of 200 solidi is payable if someone squeezes out another's eyes. Although the amount of the fine is higher than is usual in barbaric Codes, the method of imposing fines is, of course, characteristic of early Germanic laws. Let us add that the Peter of the "Exceptiones" clearly realises that the territories north of the Alps fall into two divisions, according to their relation to Roman written, and to customary, law. On one occasion he opposes the districts in which the 'most sacred laws' are in force, that is, where the authority of Imperial law is recognised, to territories where the Codes are unknown (II, 31). Another time he distinguishes between laws, that is, written laws, and the custom of the country as far as it can be discovered (secundum patriæ probabilem consuetudinem, IV, 3). We thus find in the south-east of France a distinct centre of knowledge and reflection on the subject of Roman Law, characterised by a practical tendency and developing on its own lines, although evidently influenced by intercourse with Italy. We shall remember this when we come to speak of the future development of Roman legal studies in France. The existence of this French centre of the legal revival helps to show that the more powerful and influential revival of Bologna was an event arising out of the spontaneous growth of ideas and requirements in different localities of the more civilised regions of Europe.

2. There is a second centre, as I have said, in the cities of Lombardy. The legislation of the Lombard kings, Rothari, Grimoald, Liutprand, Rachis, Ahistulf, was not abolished by the Frankish conquest of 774. Lombard Italy continued to a great extent to develop on its

own lines, although merged in the Carolingian Empire and subjected to a certain amount of Frankish legislation. When, in the eleventh century, Northern Italy advanced to prosperity and political importance, due partly to the economic progress of its cities, and partly to the activity of Emperors and Popes, the interpretation of Lombard laws in tribunals made rapid progress, and assumed the character of systematic and reflective study. We hear not only of ingenious barristers (*causidici*) and of learned judges, but of actual schools, in which rival teachers gathered pupils and expounded the materials of Lombard and Franco-Lombard law. A mine of information is supplied by the interpretation of these enactments in the school of Pavia. This interpretation finds expression, to begin with, in questions and glosses, which not only employ the comparison of texts and reasoning, but also refer more and more frequently to Roman Law. Our texts show that one of the exponents of this method of interpretation was a certain Walcausus, whom we are able to identify in charters as a judge of the Imperial court, who held office in Verona about the middle of the eleventh century. It is worth noticing that the collections of glosses on Lombard law often oppose his explanations to those of the older group of interpreters of the law. The opinions of the latter were marked with the abbreviation *a*, meaning *antiqui*, but often extended as *amentes* (the madmen), or even as *asini* (donkeys), while in the abbreviation for Walcausus, *v* is read *valentes*—the prevailing, those who get the better of it. The best insight into the method of Lombard jurisconsults is afforded by the so-called Exposition to the book of Pavia, a compilation of laws obtaining in Lombardy. It is an extended commentary based on the work of several generations of lawyers.

The authorities on the old school of Pavia, *antiqui, antiqui judices, antiqui causidici*, are referred to on seventy-two occasions. Among them, the most prominent were Bonifilius, an assessor of the Imperial courts mentioned in charters from A.D. 1014 to 1055, and Lanfranc, the famous Archbishop of Canterbury, who, in his younger days, was a conspicuous light of the school of Pavia. He left it in 1042 for Normandy, where he became a monk and later abbot of Bec, before following William the Conqueror to England. As has been shown by a careful investigation of his later theological writings, he did not consign his juridical training to oblivion even in the time of his greatness in England. Of the younger Lombard jurisconsults, the most prominent were Gualcausus (Walcausus), mentioned above, Guilelmus, and Ugo. To give you some idea of the way in which legal questions were put and controversies conducted by the Lombard doctors,

I will just refer to two of these disputes in which Lanfranc took part. Guido of Spoleto, elected emperor in 889, had enacted that in case a charter was impugned as a forgery, the notary who had drawn it up, or, if the notary were dead, the person producing the charter, should defend it by calling up witnesses and swearing to its genuineness with twelve oath-helpers. Lanfranc is reported to have had the following encounter with Bonifilius about this enactment. He asked the latter what was to be done if the notary and the witnesses were dead. Bonifilius answered, "The party producing the charter can clear it with twelve oath-helpers and two other charters (required for the verification of the notary's handwriting)." To this Lanfranc said, "Is there no other custom but this?" Bonifilius: "No." Lanfranc: "In this case the custom is against the law, as is shown by the prologue to Otto's laws, where it says that a detestable and dishonest custom, which ought not to be followed, has obtained currency in Italy." After this Bonifilius left with shame in his face and a bowed head. But Willelmus defined the meaning of the change with considerable ingenuity in the following manner. Otto's prologue had in view that some persons, greedy after other men's goods, acquired them by perjury. Therefore King Otto enacted that the plaintiff had the right to require the contention to be decided by battle. If he did not do so, the defendant, who had produced the charter, was left free to defend himself by oath-helpers. It appears from this narrative that Lanfranc considered Otto's prologue to contain a general condemnation of the procedure of swearing oaths, and Bonifilius did not know how to meet the argument drawn from the later enactment of Otto. Willelmus, however, found a way out of the difficulty by applying the words "detestable custom" (*mos detestabilis*), not to the swearing of the oath, but to the practice of perjury, so that Otto's enactment was understood as completing, and not as abolishing that of Guido. The plaintiff had the option of choosing trial by battle, but if he did not do so, the older rule about the oath held good. In an amusing exposition to Grimowald, c. 8, Lanfranc is represented as making fools of the disciples of Bonifilius by propounding to them the thorny question which of two wives had the right to a fourth part of their husband's inheritance after his death, if he had constrained his first wife to enter a monastery and married a second. The dialectician leads his interlocutors astray by putting before them six arguments of different kinds. They agree with him (*bene dixisti*) each time he brings forward one of these, and no sooner have they done so than he reproves them (*immo male*), and tacks on the opposite course, until at last he arrives at the conclusion that the second wife

cannot be considered a lawful one, and has therefore no right to the fourth part. The windings
of this dialectic exercise give rise to lengthy developments, which I cannot report here, but let
us notice that in the course of the argument,
Lanfranc not only draws on Lombard enactments, which he characteristically styles *jus
gentium*, but also juggles with a direct quotation
from the Institutes : on the strength of the law
in the Institutes, which runs "Roman citizens
contract lawful marriage," she cannot acquire
the fourth part of her husband's property. This
suggests the conclusion that the Lombard doctors
considered Roman Law as the general or common
law to which recourse must be made in all cases
where Lombard enactments provided no ground
of appeal. The rule is stated in so many words
in the Exposition to Guido, c. 4; the ancients
said that as the law did not contain any precepts
on certain questions, such cases must be decided
according to Roman Law, which is the general
law of all (*quæ omnium est generalis*). This
principle, exemplified in particular cases, is, of
course, of primary importance. It shows that
Lombard, barbarian, judges and jurisconsults
had been led by the exercise of juridical dialectics
to look to Roman Law for instruction and direction. The controversies reported by the Exposition are doubly interesting, inasmuch as
they stand in close touch with the practice of

tribunals, and at the same time manifest the beginnings of systematic teaching in law. We cannot say where and how these disputations were conducted, but the reports show that they were not simply encounters between barristers in pleading or differences of opinion between judges, but the outcome of school organisation. For this reason I do not think the designation—"Lombard doctors "—an inappropriate one. The principal place where these juridical studies were organised was Pavia, although the claims of Verona and Nonantula have also been urged.

3. As against the mixed characters of these studies in Lombardy, where Roman and Germanic Law were blended, a legal school on purely Romance ground arose in Ravenna. There are some indications as to legal studies also in Rome, but it is impossible to discover whether the legal teaching there was carried on as a special faculty. As to Ravenna, definite evidence proves that a school of jurists took an active part in the struggle between Pope Gregory VII and the Emperor Henry IV. It stood on the Emperor's side, and supported Wibert of Ravenna (Clement III), the anti-pope raised by Henry against his formidable opponent. From Ravenna, Petrus Crassus launched against Gregory VII a violent pamphlet, armed with quotations from Roman legal sources. On the other side, the fiery Cardinal Peter Damiani inveighed against the iniquitous lawyers of

Ravenna. One of Damiani's writings, composed between 1061 and 1073, is especially characteristic. It treats of the introduction into legal practice of the Roman computation of relationship. The Florentines consulted the lawyers of Ravenna, who assembled *in corpore* and pronounced in favour of the Roman computation. Damiani reproves them angrily, and speaks with scorn of the wise men of Ravenna in congregation (*Sapientes civitatis Ravennæ in unum convenientes*), of their books (the *Corpus Juris*) and their Justinian. This passage and other indications substantiate a famous account of the rise of the Bolognese school, given by Odofredus, a thirteenth-century Bolognese. According to him, the centre of legal studies was originally at Rome, but, in consequence of wars, it was transferred to Ravenna, and from Ravenna it came to Bologna.

4. The immediate occasion for the creation of the great Bolognese school was provided by the endeavours of the famous Marchioness Matilda. As a staunch supporter of Gregory VII, she wanted to counterbalance the influence of the Imperialistic school in Ravenna by establishing a centre of studies in Roman Law that would act on the papal side. The first exponent of laws in Bologna had been a certain Pepo, who taught in the last quarter of the eleventh century. He is mentioned as a doctor of laws

in a notable judgment delivered in the court of Beatrice, Duchess of Tuscany, in 1076, in which the Digest was referred to and utilised for the decision. But the man with whose literary activities the rise of the Bologna law school has been traditionally connected, is, of course, Irnerius or Guarnerius. Originally a teacher of arts, he went to Rome at the instigation of the Marchioness Matilda, and, after having studied there for some time, began to lecture on law in Bologna. This happened towards the end of the eleventh century, perhaps about 1088.

I need not dwell on the brilliant success of this teaching, and on the external circumstances attending the development of the Bologna school. It is well known that it soon became the leading university of the Middle Ages for the study of law, and that it attracted thousands of under-graduates from all countries of Europe.

I should like to characterise briefly the spirit of this revival of legal studies. It presents at bottom an application to law of the method which was employed by the new scholarship of Western Europe for the treatment of all problems of theology and science—the so-called scholastic method. The dark centuries preceding the year 1000 A.D., when learning meant merely the sal-vage of fragments of ancient knowledge, were followed by a period when organisation again appeared. The great instrument for the advancement of learning at that time was the dialectical process by which formal and universal logic analyses conceptions and constructs syllogisms. The permeation of the insufficient, fragmentary, classical texts by overwhelming logic was, in a sense, a masterly achievement, and the lawyers had more than their fair share in this work. While their fellows in the school of Divinity operated on Scripture and Canonic tradition, and the masters of arts struggled, by the help of distorted versions of Aristotle, with the rudiments of metaphysics, politics, and natural science, the lawyers exercised their dialectical acumen on a material really worthy of the name, namely, on the contents of the *Corpus Juris*. And as legal reasoning largely consists of dialectical analysis and co-ordination, they were able to produce remarkable results even at this early stage.

It is not a matter of pure chance that the text of the *Corpus Juris* received critical attention, and was restored to completeness. For the doctors of the new study, the books of Justinian were sacred books, the sources of authority from which all deductions must proceed. It is not to be wondered that they were not content with casual fragments, but made researches into its component elements, and considered it as a whole. The use of the Pisa MS. of the Digest (now in Florence) was certainly of the utmost importance

46

for the reconstitution of a good text of the most valuable part of the *Corpus Juris*. But even apart from the study of that MS., the different elements of Justinian's codification were gradually saved from oblivion, and the Bolognese Vulgate, the version made up for use in the schools, is historically of no less interest than the Littera Pisana. Irnerius himself took a prominent part in the collection of Justinian's texts by replacing the fragments of the Novellæ, hitherto quoted from Julian's Epitome, by the so-called Authenticum, a more complete Latin compilation of later date. Altogether, the critical examination of the state of the text was one of the chief preoccupations of the Bolognese scholars.

The next was literal interpretation, and in this respect the Bolognese followed in the footsteps of early mediæval literary students. They became glossators *par excellence*, although the gloss is certainly not a weapon peculiar to them. But their glosses could not well remain between the lines as explanations of single words or short remarks. They naturally spread out on the margin, where there was more room for notes, that were not merely transliterations. With Azo and Accursius they grew to be consecutive commentaries, and at that stage, the period of glossators proper comes to an end (about 1250). It covered roughly 150 years.

One of the ways in which the gloss was made

to illustrate the text was to summarise its contents in short sentences. Compilers of ancient glosses called such summaries *notabilia*. With the Bolognese they assumed a more distinct character as statements of juridical rules, and were nicknamed *Brocardica*. A collection of such *brocardica* was made in the school of Azo.

Another common expedient, employed to give a systematic view of the divisions of an intricate subject, was the *distinctio*. Starting with a general term or wide conception, it indicated the different species subordinated to it, splitting each up into its subdivisions, and following these ramifications of sense and terminology into the most minute details. To take a very simple instance, it was done in this manner :

$$\text{Iudex} \begin{cases} \text{alias electus,} \\ \text{alias compromis-} \\ \quad \text{sarius,} \end{cases} \text{alias} \begin{cases} \text{major,} \\ \text{minor,} \end{cases} \text{alias} \begin{cases} \text{ordinarius.} \\ \text{delegatus.} \end{cases}$$

This method had already been much in favour in the school of Pavia.

All these simple processes of study were subordinated to the dialectical analyses of texts, in which these were shown either to complete and support each other, or to contain gaps and contradictions. The latter case offered opportunities for the exercise of the reputed scholastic ingenuity. And here it must be noticed that the earlier doctors, though most keen and clever in their operations, generally contrive to explain the texts, while, later on, especially after Accursius, the construction of artificial arguments for its own sake begins to attract schoolmen.

In any case the dialectical analysis of texts was the great work of the school of Bologna, and in this respect it attained an excellence which we cannot refrain from admiring even now. In its first period, that of the glossators, it developed the theoretical side of teaching. It strove, according to its lights, to present as pure, clear, and complete a statement of Roman legal doctrine as possible. The mixture of Roman and barbarian elements, characteristic of the school of Pavia, and even of that of Provence, disappears. Irnerius, Placentinus, Azo, Accursius, reason as if the Lord Justinian was still holding sway over Italy, and all disputes were to be decided in his courts. The academic standpoint imposed limitations, but at the same time was a source of intellectual strength. It enabled the glossators to master thoroughly and in all directions the materials of the *Corpus Juris*. A slight but significant sign of the extent to which these scholars became familiar with the texts is shown in their manner of quoting them. Instead of referring to chapter and verse, that is quoting book, title, law, and clause, as we do now, and as was done in earlier times, the glossators, following the lead of the school of Pavia, referred to a passage by the rubric of the title, and sometimes a reference to a book. For instance, in support of the rule that no one can reclaim his property by the procedure of *condictio* from anyone but a thief, they referred to *Digest, usufructuarius quemadmodum, last law,* which, according to the modern mode of reference, would be Digest VII, 9, 12. This means, of course, that a doctor of Bologna was expected to have the entire mass of chapters' rubrics in the *Corpus* at his fingers' ends. Besides mastering the material and expounding it in a rational way, these jurists were fond of putting different cases for solution, as is done, for instance, in a tract entitled, *Quæstiones de juris subtilitatibus,* attributed to Irnerius. As in the Lombard school, they delighted in controversies, and the trend of the more important disputes has been preserved to us, notably in a work on the *Dissensiones dominorum,* and in the great summarising glosses of Azo and Accursius.

5. The school did not identify itself with any of the great political parties of the time. Though Irnerius began under the protection of the Marchioness Matilda, he changed sides after attaining success, and in the later part of his life was a palatine judge under Henry V. His successors, the four doctors — Bulgarus, Martinus, Jacobus, and Ugo — made the memorable declaration at the Roncaglia Diet of 1158 in favour of the Emperor

Barbarossa's right to tax the cities of Lombardy. In this case, however, they seem to have been actuated not so much by Ghibelline zeal as by their natural inclination to interpret the sources of Roman Law in a literal sense, and to attribute to them an actual bearing on the controversies of the twelfth century. These very doctors, however, were by no means agreed as to the limits of Imperial authority, and an anecdote of the schools tells us that when the Emperor Frederic was riding one day with Bulgarus on his right hand and Martinus on the left, he asked them whether the Emperor was not by right lord (*dominus*) of everything held by his subjects. One of the doctors, Bulgarus, had the courage to answer that he was lord in the political sense, but not in the sense of an owner. Some of the Bolognese jurists held staunchly to the Guelf party, as did, for instance, one of the most brilliant among them, Placentinus. But, of course, the natural bent of these men schooled in the law of the later empire inclined to the monarchical point of view. In any case they stood for a central authority as against feudal disruption, and although some of them made a study of feudal law, they treated it as a development of the Roman doctrine of emphyteusis.

6. The best way to obtain some insight into the intellectual work of the glossators is, I think, to examine the teaching of one of them in some

concrete cases. I should like from this point of view to dwell somewhat on the doctrine of Vacarius, who, although by no means the most brilliant or influential representative of the school, deserves our special attention as a pioneer of the new learning in England. The external facts of his career are sufficiently known. He studied Lombard and canon as well as civil law, and has written on all three branches of contemporary jurisprudence, but he was principally concerned with the teaching of Roman Law, and may be considered a fair representative of the earlier Bolognese jurists. He was attracted to England by Archbishop Theobald, taught in Canterbury and, according to Gervase's testimony, in Oxford. He was silenced for some time by Stephen, either because his teaching was considered dangerous to the authority of native legal custom, or because Stephen was jealous of the success obtained by a clerk of Archbishop Theobald, who maintained a hostile attitude towards him. Vacarius must have resumed his professional activity after an interruption of some years, and, in any case, his doctrinal influence left a deep trace in Oxford, where the students of law came to be styled *pauperistæ*, because their principal text-book was Vacarius' *Book of Poor Scholars* (*Liber pauperum*).

No complete edition of this work has ever been made, but it is sufficiently known, as several

MSS. of it have come down to us, and some extracts from his glosses have been published by Wenck and Stölzel. The *Liber pauperum* is a compilation of the Codex and of the Digest arranged for students who had not the means to acquire costly books, nor the time to make a prolonged study of Roman sources. The glosses are brief remarks inserted between the lines and on the margins. One of the earliest shows our author grappling with a difficulty in the application of the privileges of the Church concerning prescription. According to enactments of Justinian, ecclesiastical institutions were not debarred from asserting claims concerning property by the usual prescription of thirty years ; that common law period was extended for them to forty years, and the canonists asserted that the Church of Rome had a right to even a greater extension, namely, one hundred years. There was a lively controversy on the latter point among civilians, in which Vacarius did not take part, however. The Worcester MS. of his book simply gives an extract from Nov. 9 as to the hundred years' privilege of the Church of Rome, and does not go into the question how far it was abrogated by Nov. III. But our author does not fail to notice a question as to the juridical application of the privilege. Was it possible to plead the thirty years' prescription against the Church if it had acquired property from a private person who had not asserted his right within the thirty years allowed by common law ? One set of lawyers, as Vacarius' gloss tells us, replied in the negative, because no one can pass a right he does not possess. But our glossator notices also another opinion— that the privilege of the Church is derived from its own peculiar position, and was not to be made dependent on the passing of a right by an outsider. This is how I understand the short remark in Vacarius' *Liber pauperum,* and it may serve as an example of the juridical queries which constantly presented themselves to the attentive student of Roman legal authorities.

The next section, devoted to a commentary on D. i, 3, intituled " on laws, enactments, decrees of the senate and long custom "—*de legibus, constitutionibus, senatus consultis et longa consuetudine),* is of greater general interest ; it treats, according to an explanatory gloss, of *laws about laws,* which are contrasted with laws about business matters *(leges legum—leges negociorum).* Vacarius treads here on ground occupied by the most vital problems of jurisprudence. The glossators were greatly exercised by the fundamental question of the relation between law and equity. I have already had occasion to notice the radical point of view of the *Exceptiones Petri.* The author of this Provençal text-book does not scruple to tread under foot positive rules of law which seem to him obsolete or contrary to equity.

And he is by no means alone in taking up such a position. The author of a tract on subtle questions of law of Irnerius describes graphically in his prologue a wall on which are engraved texts of law. Honourable men in great numbers frequently approach this wall and study the texts diligently, so that enactments which do not conform with equity may be taken as can-celled. In the manual of a MS. of Troyes (*Summa Trecensis*),* representing one of the first steps in the jurisprudence of the epoch of glossators, we are told that laws have to be interpreted in a humane way, so that their meaning may be preserved, and there should be no discrepancy with equity ; the precepts of laws should be admitted only if they tally with equity (*Summa Trecensis*, I, 14, §§ 6, 7). On the other hand, Irnerius himself, as a genuine gloss of his testifies, saw a danger in such a wide power to modify law on the part of the judge.† He considers equity as the mere enunciation of a principle of justice, whereas law propounds the same principle as the expression of a will, that is, with a certain admixture of authority. Both differ considerably through the weakness of human nature ; law contains partly more and partly less than is ordained by equity. They differ also in many other ways, and the interpretation of their dis-crepancies, if it is to have force of law, appertains

* Fitting attributes it to Irnerius. † App. IV.

to sovereigns only. From what we learn of the teaching of Bulgarus, he stood up for a stricter interpretation of law, while Martinus and his pupil, Placentinus, inclined towards more lax interpretation.

It is interesting to see that Vacarius' position in this controversy is indicated by a short but interesting gloss.* He starts from the doctrine that the Emperor is the only originator and interpreter of law. In his case lawgiving is the outcome of his will, while others, that is, subordinate magistrates and judges, may have to lay down the law from necessity. This being so, one need not wonder at the maxim that the sovereign is not bound by the law (*legibus solutus*); law itself is the creation of his will. And further, when a judge interprets law, his interpretation holds good merely in the case of litigants before him, and in so far as they have no legal remedy at hand against his decision. Thus interpretation modifying the legal rule itself is reserved to the action of the legislator, and not conceded to the judge. Any discrepancy between equity and law has therefore to be removed by legislative means, while the power of the judge does not reach further than the dispute immediately in hand.

The same reverential attitude towards sovereign authority underlies the teaching of Vacarius on legal custom. The glossators were again divided

* App. V.

on this point. According to one view the people, having surrendered its legislative power to the Emperor, custom is subordinated to law, and the latter cannot be repealed even by disuse. From another point of view, popular custom appears as the survival of the legislative authority of the people, and this justifies the modification of express laws by custom. A gloss of Vacarius bears on this difference of opinion. His contention is that things are generally dissolved by the same process by which they have been created. An enactment may be made, and will hold good even against the wish and protest of the people. Therefore it cannot be abrogated by custom, unless the people has resumed Imperial authority and power by depriving the sovereign of them. The last words contemplate a possible resumption of power by the people—an interesting conception by no means uncommon during the Middle Ages. But this part of the doctrine is not developed further, whereas the initial remarks are in complete harmony with the part assigned by Vacarius to the legislative omnipotence of the sovereign.

The above-mentioned passages may be sufficient to show what a lively intercourse of ideas was taking place among these twelfth-century scholars. Their discussions were conducted very much on academic lines, but it is clear that the interests of actual life were by no means without influence on the setting and solution of their problems. Judicial interpretation, the influence of custom, the part played by the idea of sovereignty, in the formation of law—all these questions had, besides their intrinsic jurisprudential value, a special interest for men who were moving in a society where the elements of law and political order had to be, as it were, discovered anew. The theorists framed their definitions and distinctions in too rigid a manner ; yet they helped materially to disentangle the general conceptions of law from the chaotic uncertainty of a blind struggle for existence.

LECTURE III

ROMAN LAW IN FRANCE

Authorities : Brachylogus juris civilis, ed. *Böcking*, 1829 ; Lo Codi, ed. *H. Fitting* und *H. Suchier*, 1906 ; *E. Litten*, Ueber lo Codi und Seine Stellung in der Entwickelung des Culpa—Problems in the Mélanges, Fitting, II, 1908 ; *A. Tardif*, Histoire des Sources du droit français; Origines romaines, 1890; *J. Brissaud*, Histoire du droit français, 1899 ; *P. Viollet*, Histoire du droit civil français, 1905 ; *Esmein*, Histoire du droit français, 8 éd. 1907 ; *P. Viollet*, Les établissements de St. Louis, I–IV, 1881–6 ; *Ch. Guiraud*, Essai sur l'histoire du droit français au moyen âge, 1846 ; *Beaumanoir*, Coutume de Beauvaisis, ed. *Salmon*, I, II, 1899 ; *P. Van Wetter*, Le droit romain et Beaumanoir in the Mélanges, Fitting, II, 1908 ; *Éd. Meynial*, Des renonciations au moyen âge et dans notre ancien droit, in the Nouvelle Revue historique de droit français et étranger, 1900, 1901, 1902, 1904 ; *Bordier*, Philippe de Remi, sire de Beaumanoir, 1869.

1. I HAVE already had occasion to notice several facts which show that Italy was by no means the only country in which signs of a revival of civilisation appeared in the eleventh century. France was also on the way towards new ideals of culture and learning. If Italian life was preparing for the rise of Bologna, French life was gathering strength for the glory of the University of Paris. The course of the latter was dedicated to the arts, divinity, and canon

law, but the great scholastic movement, consisting in the concentration of studies, was nowhere more powerful than in Paris, and it could not but react on legal learning. It showed a growth of intellectual power which by itself was bound to benefit indirectly the study of laws. And indeed, we find many products of French scholarship dedicated to law at the same critical period when the Italian school was gradually taking shape. Besides the *Exceptiones Petri*, already mentioned above, I should like to call attention to the work of Ivo of Chartres (about 1100). His *Decretum* and his *Panormita* show a minute acquaintance with Roman legal sources and more especially with Justinian's codification. Another valuable legal book of French origin is the *Brachylogus juris civilis*, a very clear and learned manual for the teaching of Roman Law, probably composed in the first quarter of the twelfth century ; though showing traces of the influence of the glossators, it still remains original in its method of arranging material and stating rules.

The most interesting contribution of France to the revival of Roman Law is the recently discovered summary of Justinian's Code, compiled for the use of judges in Provence, the so-called *Lo Codi*. Like the *Exceptiones Petri*, it originated in the south-eastern corner of France, probably in Arles, which in the twelfth century was a dependency of the Empire. An allusion to the possible capture of Fraga, a fortified town in the March of Barcelona, enables us to fix the date of its composition as about 1149. Certain Provençal expressions occur in the *Exceptiones Petri*, but *Lo Codi* was written entirely in the Provençal language, and presents therefore the first treatise on Roman Law composed in a native dialect. The Provençal text has not been published yet, but Professor Suchier of the University of Halle is preparing an edition of it. A Latin translation, made by Ricardus Pisanus some time before 1162, is already in our hands, thanks to the industry of Professor Hermann Fitting, the leading representative of the study of Roman Law in the Middle Ages.

Lo Codi stands already under the influence of the glossators. It follows closely a summary of the Codex extant in a MS. of Troyes (*Summa Trecensis*) and attributed by Fitting to Irnerius himself. The authorship of Irnerius cannot be proved, but the *Summa Trecensis* is, in any case, a fair sample of an early glossator's work. The compilers of the Codex have also utilised a *Summa Codicis* of *Rogerus*, a glossator of the third generation. It seems, in fact, that Rogerus personally took part in the compilation of the *Codi*. Yet the *Codi* has distinctive features which on the one hand distinguish it from the Bolognese books, and on the other hand connect it with the tradition of the *Exceptiones Petri*. It is written not for academic use, but for the courts, and more particularly for laymen acting as presiding judges or arbitrators ; it is absolutely free from pedantry or abstruse argument ; it aims chiefly at clearness, and at easy access in case of reference. Cases likely to occur in common practice are constantly put. *Lo Codi* is, in short, a manual for immediate use, somewhat resembling the books of reference of modern justices of the peace. I will give one or two instances in illustration of its treatment of the subject.

The rules as to the responsibility of a person using goods belonging to another greatly exercised the ingenuity of Roman lawyers. The borrower was, of course, answerable for fraudulent misuse (*dolus*), but how far was he answerable for negligence (*culpa*) ? Nerva, as reported by Celsus, had laid down that gross negligence (*culpa latior*) is equivalent to fraud, and constitutes a breach of good faith. But what is to be taken as the measure of gross negligence ? The *Codi* points to some palpable absurdities to illustrate the general meaning of gross negligence. It arises when a person thinks that what is noxious to everyone else is innocuous to him, as, for example, if I leave a book out in the rain and do not consider that it is sure to be damaged, or if I lead a horse, entrusted to my care, by places that I know to be the haunts of robbers and thieves. Such acts constitute gross negligence, and I must compensate for any damages resulting from it. But it is not sufficient to point to extreme absurdities. In practice, much will depend on the standard of reasonableness. And although the *Codi* does not follow the Roman lawyers in tracing minutely the differences between *culpa, culpa latior,* and *dolus,* it is very careful to set up a standard of reasonable care and to make it as practical as possible. Classical jurisconsults were divided : some held that a *minimum* of average care was sufficient to avoid direct responsibility for damage, others that the party to a contract was bound to exercise a high degree of diligence, to act as a good householder (*bonus paterfamilias*) and as a wise man (*sapiens*) would have done under the circumstances. The compilation of Justinian and the early glossators did not pay much attention to the controversy, and failed to provide definite rules for the guidance of practitioners. Not so the *Codi.* From its eminently practical standpoint, the question as to the proper standard was of much greater importance than the abstract derivation of *culpa.* It declares for a standard of high efficiency : it amounts to culpable negligence if I have not taken care of borrowed goods as a wise man would have done (*sicut faceret aliquis sapiens homo,* IV, 69, 9 ; cf. IV, 55, 3).

Let us take another instance, showing to what extent the abstract doctrines of Roman Law were influenced by customary rules and local conditions. In the treatment of damages occasioned to someone by another person's fraud or deceit (*fraude vel inganno*, II, 10), the *Codi* follows, in a general way, the doctrine laid down in Justinian's Code, II, 20. But it introduces variations in point of detail. It starts from an important distinction. If the deceiver induced the aggrieved party to enter into an unsound transaction, as, for example, to make a contract on the strength of false information, the contract must be rescinded at the request of the aggrieved party. If I have sold goods to a man who has deceived me as to the price, I may claim the difference between the diminished price and the fair value. If I did not wish to sell at all and have been induced thereto by fraud, the sale is of no effect whatever. Should fraud be employed without any reference to a contract, compensation must be made if the damage done is considerable—not less than two byzantes. In insignificant cases no action is allowed, but there may be important cases in which indemnity ought to be granted. For instance, a person called his brother to his death-bed and said to him, "Brother, be you my heir, and if you are not my heir, my wife shall be." After the death of the testator, the widow circumvented the rightful heir by fraudulently persuading him not to accept a ruinous inheritance. When he followed her advice she took the inheritance and holds it. This is a case for indemnity, although not connected with any particular contract. The whole setting of the case and of the distinctions is evidently coloured by actual practice, and is not merely copied from Justinian's Code or from the summaries of the glossators.

2. We have thus in the Provençal *Codi* an excellent example of the intelligent and practical use of Roman Law in a region where this law was recognised as the principal legal authority. But the influence of Roman sources stretched much further. It affected materially the state of the law in parts of France governed by customary laws derived to a large extent from German tradition. Here the process of transformation is especially suggestive. It does not start with the acceptance of an external authority from which all changes in detail should be derived, but from a kind of struggle for existence between concrete rules and institutions of German and of Roman origin.

Naturally the initial move in this case came from the spread of knowledge. It was necessary to study Roman Law before applying it, and it is material from this point of view that the Bolognese school not only attracted foreigners, and, among them, many Frenchmen, but also that it sent forth disciples into France. One of the most brilliant glossators, Placentinus, disgusted with Bologna, became a famous teacher of the law school at Montpellier. The legal faculty there was situated in the "*pays de droit écrit,*" in the region dominated by Roman Law, but it also served as an influential centre for the rest of France. There can be no doubt that the rise of this rival of Bologna on French soil greatly contributed to the development of jurisprudence, and to the progress of law itself, during the eventful centuries when both England and France evolved the fundamental institutions of their national law. Later on, the school of Orléans, organised in 1312 by Philip IV, became the authoritative representative of legal teaching in the "*pays de droit coutumier,*" but this official step had been prepared by the activity of legal writers and by academic influence, first in Montpellier and then in Orléans itself.

The reign of St. Louis is as conspicuous for the progress of legal institutions as for its two crusades and its brilliant feats of chivalry. Trial by battle is relegated to the background in the Royal courts, and the production of evidence takes its place, while the organisation of the Parlement of Paris assumes a systematic and well-developed form. To this juridical revival two principal causes can be assigned—the growth of royal authority and a diligent study of Law. As we are concerned with the latter, let us notice the appearance of the *Conseil à un ami* (advice to a friend) of Philip of Fontaines, *bailli* of Vermandois.

ROMAN LAW IN FRANCE

His work testifies to an eager interest in, and a very poor understanding of, written law. Fontaines simply copies passages from the Digest and from the Institutes without being able to co-ordinate or interpret them. More curious is a production of the Orléans school, the *Book of Justice and Pleading* (*le livre de justice et de plaid*). Of its 342 clauses, 197 are borrowed from Roman sources, while the rest are of customary origin. The unknown author, perhaps a professor of the Orléans school, tries to enliven his dry subject by numerous references to the sayings and doings of the great personages of his time ; but these references turn out to be fictitious—somewhat resembling similar references to King Alfred and Anglo-Saxon judges in the English *Mirror of Justices*. A passage from Ulpian appears, for example, under the name of King Louis himself, and quotations attributed to Renaut de Tricot, Geoffrey de la Chapelle, and other worthies, are not more genuine.

Next comes a private compilation which achieved a great reputation and influence under the name of the *Établissements de Saint Louis*. Only its first nine chapters are drawn from the Ordinances of St. Louis. The other paragraphs of the first book present a statement of a custom of Touraine-Anjou, while the second book consists of a custom of the Orléanais. The compiler has patched these two records of customary law with extracts from Justinian's *Corpus Juris*, but even when these are removed, the influence of Roman rules remains distinctly traceable, especially in the Orléans custom.

3. The most interesting document of French juridical revival under the influence of Roman Law is the remarkable *Coutume de Beauvaisis*, compiled by Philippe de Rémi, Sire de Beaumanoir, between 1279 and 1283, some ten or fifteen years later than Bracton's great treatise on the Common Law of England. Beaumanoir had been *bailli*, that is, judge and deputy governor, of the county of Clermont in Beauvaisis, which belonged to Robert de Clermont, the sixth son of St. Louis. He was a man of extraordinary ability, learning, and varied experience. He had served in England in his early youth and has left not only the juridical tract already mentioned, but poetry, including a poetical romance describing the adventures of a French knight, Jehan, and a fair lady of Oxford, Blonde d'Oxford. His originality of mind did not fail him when he came to treat of legal topics, and his *Coutume de Beauvaisis* is one of the most refreshing legal treatises in existence. He knew his Roman Law thoroughly, and used it with the freedom and dexterity of one who had mastered its contents and was not a slave to its superior authority.

In order to judge of the influence exerted by Roman Law on the legal usage of Northern France, we can hardly do better than consider in some detail the teaching of Beaumanoir on a few subjects of legal doctrine.

Beaumanoir's prologue * to his work is well worth notice. He does not hope to impress the reader by his personal authority, and even conceals his name until the end of the book, so that the good wine he offers may not be left untasted because of its poor " *étiquette.*" We need not take the author's modesty too literally, but this much is certain : he sets himself a carefully restricted and unambitious aim. He wants to give primarily the substance of local custom in his own place—Clermont in Beauvaisis, because he is well acquainted with it, while the further he goes from his district, the less he can vouch for the accuracy of his knowledge. Therefore, if he can base his information on actual judgments or ascertainable custom of Clermont, he will rely first of all on them, and only when doubts arise as to local custom, will he turn to the custom of neighbouring lordships or even to the common law of the kingdom of France. The point of view is characteristic of a French lawyer of a period which may still be called feudal. It is exactly opposed to the method of Bracton, who, strong in the judicial authority of Royal courts, sets out to describe the common law of England and refers to local custom only as a subordinate source

* App. VI.

of information. This being so, what is the meaning attached to the term "common law" by
Beaumanoir ? It occurs several times in his
treatise, and can only mean legal rules generally
accepted throughout the realm of France, for
example, the rule that a husband disposes of his
wife's property during their married life. This is
not a rule especially expressed in Beauvaisis custom or established in the tribunal of Clermont,
nor is it a rule in strict correspondence with
Justinian's law, but is the view generally prevailing in France, and, I presume, acted upon by
Royal courts such as the Parlement of Paris (cf.
§ 552 on wardship). From this and other instances it is clear that Beaumanoir's use of the
term is a much more lax one than that of Bracton.
Whereas for the latter the common law of England is primarily substantiated and exemplified
by the decisions of the Royal courts of justice,
the French jurists seem to look more to the
comparative evidence of divers customs, amount-
ing to what might be termed a law common to all
French territories. Some of the MSS. of Beaumanoir have actually expressed as much in the
text of the passage in question. An appeal to the
decision of Royal courts, of the Parlement of
Paris, is not excluded, but is not indicated as
necessary (cf. § 374). As for a possible reference
to Roman Law, it cannot have been the meaning
of the author to speak of it as the general or

common law in the same sense as, for instance, Lombard jurists had done. Roman Law as such was not recognised within the territory of customary law. It applied only when it had been accepted by the jurisprudence of local courts, by local custom, or general custom. This seems clearly proved by two considerations ; firstly, by an express declaration that reasonable men ought to follow their own customs and not " ancient laws " of which they do not know enough ; and, secondly, by the fact that Beaumanoir's prologue is constructed on the same lines as a passage of Julian's in the Digest, but that he intentionally differs from it as to the decisive point. Where Julian has recourse to the Law of Rome, Beaumanoir says, " common law of the kingdom of France," or " the customs of France."

4. I dwell on the analysis of this prologue because it affords the best clue to the interpretation of Beaumanoir's references to Roman Law. He does not accept them on authority, and yet he draws constantly on Roman rules in so far as they have been already accepted by French legal custom or jurisprudence. Consequently, he never once quotes from Roman books, and yet his expressions frequently follow the exact wording of these same books. To put it shortly, he deals largely, not with written law itself, but with customary law partly derived from Roman origins. A good illustration is provided by his

chapters on the so-called *renunciations*, on clauses inserted in charters for the express purpose of renouncing a possible appeal to some legal rule or expedient of pleading. A number of purely Roman remedies are guarded against, as, for example, the *exceptio pecuniæ non numeratæ*, or the complaint that a vendor has obtained less than half value for his property. It is evident, however, that Beaumanoir did not compose for himself the list of all these "renunciations." He simply took the customary formulæ which had made their way into the region of customary law in the North from the region of written law in the South, where they had a much more real meaning (§§ 1094-1098). This makes his references to Roman Law only the more interesting ; they depend not on his personal taste, but on a process of acceptance or reception effected by the legal custom and jurisprudence of the age.

Some of the principal points worked out by thirteenth-century jurisprudence concerned forms of procedure. It was a matter of importance to settle in what manner and order legal remedies should be granted, claims framed, and defences against them allowed by the courts. Unless these and similar procedural points were definitely worked out, no discussion as to substantive rights could avail. The importance of procedure as a framework for material law was further enhanced by the very complicated nature of jurisdiction, the intermixture of feudal justice of various degrees, on the one hand, and of lay courts and courts Christian on the other. These difficulties presented themselves to English lawyers as early as the twelfth century, in the time of Henry II, while in France they only began to be cleared up one hundred years later, under St. Louis and his successors. And it is evident from Beaumanoir's treatise that an acquaintance with Roman terms and forms of procedure greatly facilitated the task of French lawyers in this respect. The beginning of his exposition on stages in pleading illustrates this point (ch. vi). Our author notices expressly that clerks, learned ecclesiastics, have at their disposal very suitable expressions borrowed from Latin speech, but laymen do not understand these terms when put in French. They have consequently to be explained to the latter, and they may be used in lay courts, as it were, in a vernacular guise. An action begins with a *demande* (a bill of petition), corresponding to the *libellus* of the clerks. The *libellus conventionis* of the libellary process of later Roman Law is alluded to. Beaumanoir does not dwell on the *libellus responsionis* of the defendant (*Niance de fait*, cf. § 257), but proceeds to point out the pleas which may be brought forward in answer to the allegations of the plaintiff. These are styled *exceptions*, as in Roman procedure. The plaintiff may oppose them by *replications*,

again as in a tribunal administering justice according to the *Corpus Juris*. But here the similarity
ceases. The Romans admitted further pleadings
on both sides, duplications, triplications, etc.,
and the courts Christian followed their example in
this. Not so the lay courts. The process was
simplified ; each party could plead in bar once
only. After that, issue must be joined on questions of fact. The context, in which the doctrine
is expounded, makes it probable that the Romanistic views were passed over to the courts of
customary law through the channel of ecclesiastical
tribunals. In the same way we find in the *Coutume
de Beauvaisis* (as well as in the *Établissements de
St. Louis*) Justinian's classification of actions into
personal, real, and mixed ; the first aiming at
enforcing obligations, the second directed towards
obtaining ownership of things, and the third
starting from an obligation but resulting in
claims as to things (§§ 228–230, cf. Inst. IV, 6,
§§ 1, 2, 20). In this case there is no need to assume
the influence of Canon law. The distinctions were
well known and frequently treated in all schools
where law was taught.

A subject of much importance to all lawyers,
and especially to lawyers of this period, was the
very fundamental distinction between ownership
and possession, and its effects on legal procedure.
In ancient German law, when private ownership
of land was greatly restricted, quarrels as to

ownership occurred chiefly between clans, townships, ecclesiastical institutions, etc., and were treated as fundamentally different from the assertions of individual claims. On the other hand, rights of protected occupation and possession arose easily, and were based on the application of labour to a particular plot of land. If a man was suffered to settle on and to cultivate a piece of land for a year and a day, he could claim the protection of the courts for his labour and occupation. This is the origin of the peculiar German *"usucaption"* by a year and a day. It is derived from the effective short - period cultivation of an otherwise unreclaimed plot. This mode of *"usucaption"* is clearly set forth in the customal of Touraine-Anjou enrolled in the first book of the *Établissements* (I, 163), and it occurs also in Beaumanoir's treatise. "The user of one year and a day is sufficient to acquire seisin (protected possession), as when a man holds ploughed land, or a vineyard, or another piece of inheritance (land) and takes the fruits of it for a year and a day. Should anyone come then and prevent him, the lord ought to remove the obstacle, until he has lost the land in a trial for ownership " (§ 685 ; cf. 955). Apart from the peculiarly short period of " *usucaption,*" we notice here the definite wish of the authorities to protect seisin as a *prima facie* ground for occupying and using land. Several distinct actions sprang from this far - reaching principle. The well - known remedy of the English courts—the action of Novel Disseisin—is not unknown in French law, but it comes into being rather late by a Royal Ordinance of 1277 (§§ 958, 959). Customary procedure admitted also of a plaint, or a complaint, as they said in France, to the lord of the country against violent interruption of peaceful possession, and it was sufficient that this should have lasted for a year and a day. On the other hand, Canon law had borrowed from Roman Law a process which, through the channel of ecclesiastical jurisdiction, obtained access into provincial customals, as, for instance, into the Orléans one. In this case an entirely different theory of acquiring possession was deemed necessary. A person disturbed in the peaceful enjoyment of a plot could bring an action asking for a *réintegrande*, but the court when deciding the question of possession would require one of at least ten years if reasonable ground for it was shown, and one of thirty years if no specific ground was stated. We find the teaching as to ten and thirty years' prescription clearly stated by Beaumanoir, and he advises his readers to try for seisin by prescription before venturing on the much more difficult plea of ownership. First get your seisin, and then prove ownership if you can (§ 199).

From this point of view of the "beatitude of seisin," (*beati possidentes*) both the Orléans cus-

tomal and Beaumanoir lay great stress on a rule
which was expressed by the formula—*le mort
saisit le vif*. This does not mean that the dead
man clutches the one alive, but that the seisin of
the land or inheritance passes from the dead man,
the ancestor, to the living man, the successor.
It is a short and more striking way of saying that
the heir has no need to prove his title to land :
he is protected by the seisin of his predecessor.
The question turns on inheritance, and not on
title to property. Here again we are on firm
Roman ground.

The technical character of these rules must not
conceal from us their great social importance.
The elaboration of the doctrine of seisin, protected possession, with all its eventualities and
ramifications, made it possible to avoid the
tangle of feudal claims, and, what is more, to
establish a *prima facie* legal order where violence
and casual appropriation had reigned supreme.
The check put on Novel Disseisin was a fair test
of the efficiency and social value of the State.
When the protection of seisin had been achieved,
the disentanglement of fundamental rights could
follow. And the part played by Roman distinctions and rules in this process was considerable.

5. In matters concerning family law, the influence of Roman conceptions is not so obvious,
because some of the latter remained archaic,
as, for instance, the *patria potestas*, even in its

mitigated form. There was little to choose between Germanic and Romance custom in regard to the authority of the father and the privileged position of the male sex in legal arrangements of all kinds. On the other hand, special tenacity was evinced in the retaining of ancient native custom in the branch of law that treats of some of the forms of kinship. We find, therefore in the Beauvaisis customal such institutions as the *retrait lignager*, the right of redeeming goods alienated by a relative, the German dower—the portion settled on the wife out of the property of the husband's family, etc.

A very important departure is established by the admission of the mother to the guardianship of her child under age (§ 629 ; cf. Nov. 118). This, of course, ran entirely counter to ancient Germanic, and indeed to ancient Roman, ideas. It is not impossible that we have to do here not with a principle borrowed from Justinian's law, but with an indigenous evolution of legal conceptions.

In chapter 640, Beaumanoir discusses the responsibilities of parents for crimes committed by their children. According to this view, the father should pay the fine incurred, if the children are under his patronage (*mainburnie*). Such a child has nothing of his own, whether he be of age or under age. If the father or the mother desire to avoid responsibility, they must place their children out of their power (*main*) and patronage (*mainburnie*), and divide bread and broth with them (*pain et pot*). This teaching presents a quaint combination of terms—*main* corresponds to the Roman *manus* in the sense of power, authority, while *mainburnie* is a corruption of the Germanic *mundeburdis*. The vital points of the doctrine are, however, that children dwelling with their parents round the same kettle, even when of age, are not considered independent persons in the sense of having property of their own—a very positive expression of the unity of the joint household. The latter was, of course, very characteristic of Germanic archaic custom, as well as of Roman. The *Corpus Juris* shows that a person, who had attained full age, remains in the power of the father unless emancipated by him, the separation of the households and property rights being commonly effected by the marriage of the son.

Another department of the law strongly affected by Roman influence was the law of contract. This subject grows in importance with the development of intercourse, and, naturally enough, Roman rules were greatly in advance in this respect, as compared with the customs of barbarian communities. Besides, the circumstances under which obligations arise, are enforced, or declared invalid, vary considerably, and give occasion to much casuistry. Barristers and judges had therefore a greater latitude in bringing forward personal views, and in drawing on Roman juridical sources to support them. The definition of partnership (*compagnie*), for example, is borrowed from Inst. III, 25, §§ 1, 2. Beaumanoir especially wanted to impress his readers with the idea that it was by no means necessary for partners to contribute equal pecuniary shares to obtain equal shares in the profits. He could not do better for that purpose than refer to the passage in the Institutes.

In the analysis of contracts created by order (*mandatum*) a nice point occurs in connection with the personal character of the order. It is not difficult to see that if the person giving the order changes his mind and countermands it in time, the contract does not hold good. It is also clear that if the counter-order does not reach the agent and the latter executes the order in good faith as given to him, the principal is held by it. But what is to happen if the principal dies ? As the agent represents his person, the agreement falls to the ground, and the heir is not bound by the obligation. But one eventuality must in fairness be guarded against. If the heir has obtained some profit by the execution of the order, he cannot repudiate the obligation. Thus Beaumanoir follows Institutes III, 26, §§ 9, 10, in all its windings (§§ 810, 811).

I need not pursue further the examination

of the traces of Roman influence in Beaumanoir's text. What has been said seems more than sufficient to show how great that influence was. It was conditioned by the superiority of Roman legal rules in their struggle with corresponding, but not identical, conceptions of Germanic origin. The influx of Roman doctrine produced neither a haphazard collection of fragments nor wholesale copying and complete subordination in form and contents. It led rather to an intelligent "reception," if I may use this term commonly employed by German scholars. In other cases, Roman views were modified, combined with native ideas, or entirely rejected. And when one meets with a personality such as Beaumanoir, one comes to understand better in what way the process took place.

6. But I must not leave the subject without calling attention to one peculiarity in this psychological side of "reception." It happened not unfrequently that the practitioner or the learned judge, who were the chief agents in the process, picked out one or the other doctrine not in its proper and logical sense, but in order to confirm or to prove some opinion of their own, which possibly did not fit in exactly with the concrete rule brought forward to support it. Take, for instance, the famous maxim, *quod principi placuit legis habet vigorem* (Inst. I, 1, 2, § 6). Beaumanoir quotes it expressly in his paragraph 1103. But

it is certainly not the generally constitutional
import of this doctrine that he wishes to ac-
climatise in the France of his day. It were odd
indeed if he wanted to do so at the end of the
thirteenth century, in the time of Philip the Fair,
a few years before that King brought together
with considerable difficulty the first more or
less complete assembly of the estates of his
realm. No ; Beaumanoir makes use of this
famous maxim to give authority to a statement as
to the right of a king, starting on an expedition
or a crusade, to suspend the fulfilment of obligations for knights joining his army. In this
mediæval guise the saying of Roman jurists is
hardly recognisable, but we need not accuse
the *bailli* of Clermont of ignorance or misrepre-
sentation ; he simply made use of this Roman
plank to build a platform of his own.

Another curious case in point turns on the
use made by Beaumanoir of the principle of
the *res judicata* : * when judgment has been
delivered in a case, it ought not to be reversed
in the same court. In the absence of such a
rule litigation would have been endless. The
Romans recognised the rule in theory, and con-
sistently put it into practice. So does Beaumanoir
—he states it in his thirty-first clause, but he
gives it a peculiar twist. The one judgment
aimed at by the *res judicata* rule is, for him, the

* App. VII.

judgment of the court of the lord with its full complement of assessors, peers, or *prud'hommes*, according to mediæval phraseology. From such decisions are to be distinguished those taken by the *bailli* himself as sole judge—in cases sufficiently clear and admitting of reference to custom. Such decisions are not judgments. Why should our jurist have recourse to such an ambiguous play with words ? Two reasons may be stated. Firstly, he wanted to enlarge the scope of the personal jurisdiction of the *bailli* untrammelled by assessors. Secondly, his distinction was made to allow of reconsideration in some cases which the *bailli* found after all to be too difficult, by bringing them before the full court, without prejudice to the *res judicata* rule. In any case, we must accustom ourselves not to treat our mediæval lawyer's references to Roman texts in too strict and pedantic a manner. His object was not to present us with a faultless commentary on the *Corpus Juris*, but to make use of some of the Roman doctrines for his own purpose as a wise judge of France.

LECTURE IV

ROMAN LAW IN ENGLAND

Authorities : *Pollock and Maitland*, History of English Law, I, II ; *W. S. Holdsworth*, History of English Law, II, III, 1909 ; *Stubbs*, Lectures on Mediæval and Modern History ; *Selden*, Dissertatio ad Fletam ; *Maitland*, Bracton's Notebook, 1888 ; *Marcel Fournier*, L'Église et le droit romain au XIII siècle, in the Nouvelle Revue historique de droit français et étranger, 1890 ; *E. Caillemer*, Le droit civil dans les provinces Anglo-Normandes au XII siècle, 1883 ; *Glanvill*, De legibus et consuetudinibus Angliæ ; *Bracton*, De legibus Angliæ ; *Güterbogk*, Henricus de Bracton und Sein Verhältniss zum römisches Recht ; *F. W. Maitland*, Bracton and Azo ; Selden Society, VIII, 1894 ; *P. Vinogradoff*, Villainage in England, 1892 ; *James Williams*, Latin Maxims in English Law, Law Magazine and Review, 1895, August.

I. CIVIL law did not become a constituent element of English common law acknowledged and enforced by the courts, but it exercised a potent influence on the formation of legal doctrines during the critical twelfth and thirteenth centuries, when the foundations of common law were laid. Indeed the teaching of Roman Law inaugurated by Vacarius seemed for some time to carry everything before it. No school was more popular in Oxford at the close of the twelfth century than the school of legists. The tide was stemmed to some extent by powerful

84

agencies acting in other directions. The Church realised that its predominance was threatened by the spread of secular learning in the field of law ; Canon law was more sharply differentiated from civil jurisprudence, and it began to oppose the latter in its striving towards juridical supremacy. A bull of Honorius III (Super Speculam, A.D. 1217), and another of Innocent IV (Dolentes, A.D. 1259) were directed against the teaching of Roman Law in Paris and in "neighbouring countries." On the other hand, there grew up a national opposition against cosmopolitan doctrines which finds a definite expression in many facts. In 1234 Henry III forbade the teaching of Civil law in London, while in 1236 the great men of England, assembled at Merton, declared against any modification of English custom by foreign views in the treatment of bastardy (*Nolumus leges Angliæ mutari*).

Nevertheless, the teaching of Roman Law was never discontinued at the principal seats of learning in England. The canonists themselves frequently referred to its sources, as is shown, for instance, by the *Golden Text-Book* (*Summa aurea*) of the Oxford professor, William of Drogheda (thirteenth century). The study of Roman Law in Cambridge can be traced from this very thirteenth century, which witnessed so many declarations of the powers that be against its introduction. It was used at both universities and in other minor centres of learning as a kind of "general jurisprudence," and, as such, it exerted considerable, though indirect, influence on the practice of common law.

Turning to the results of this study in England, we have to notice, firstly, its bearing on the principal juridical doctrine evolved during the twelfth century, namely, on the doctrine of seisin, and the means of protecting it. The age of Henry II has left a profound mark in this respect by formulating the point of view of possession, and providing adequate remedies for its protection in the King's courts. As we have seen, the French lawyers were much concerned with this aspect of jurisprudence in the thirteenth century, and so were the English in the twelfth. A point in which the influence of Roman Law is clearly traceable concerns the action itself by which possession was protected. The famous writ of Novel Disseisin—introduced by Henry II's lawyers, appears as a secular variation of the canonistic action of spoliation (*actio spolii*), and this again has evidently sprung from the Roman interdict "unde vi."

To what extent the English view of seisin was coloured by Roman teaching on possession may also be gathered among other things from Glanvill's treatment of the gage of land. He admits of the transfer of land from the debtor to the creditor with the object of providing a security for debt and interest, but he fails to recognise any distinct "estate" of the creditor in land transferred in such a way. The possession of the debtor remains legally intact, and the relation of the creditor is considered as a mere matter of fact devoid of juridical essence ; it may be interrupted by the legal tenant, should the latter not be afraid of exposing himself to reprisals in the shape of a personal action.

Probably at the same time with Glanvill's treatise, William Longchamp, a Norman peasant who was to become Bishop of Durham and Regent of England in the reign of Richard Cœur-de-Lion, composed his *Practice of Laws and Decrees* (*Practica legum et decretorum*). It is a short manual of procedure based on civil as well as on canon law, and intended for use primarily in the French possessions of the English Crown. As the career of the writer demonstrates, however, there was no sharp cleavage between the English and the French parts of the Plantagenets' dominions. At the fair of Lagny in Bresse, which is casually mentioned in the tract, English merchants were so numerous that one of the streets got its name from them (*vicus Anglicus*).

The teaching of the *practica* may well have influenced contemporary English lawyers on one or two important occasions. There was, for instance, a great controversy among the jurists of the time about the framing of an action. An authoritative glossator, Placentinus, held that it was not necessary to formulate an action in accordance with strict terms ; the plaintiff might be allowed to state his claim in general expressions. Other doctors, such as Johannes Bassianus and Azo, disputed this and required the presentation of claims according to technical forms. William Longchamp's "practice" urges the necessity of definite formulæ of actions, and it may be considered in this respect as introducing the theory of strict writs adhered to by common law.

2. The most important English contribution to Romanesque jurisprudence, however, is contained in Bracton's work on the Laws and Customs of England. Although this famous book was primarily written for the instruction of practical lawyers, and its most valuable chapters are based on the case law of Henry III's age, it opens with a comprehensive introduction chiefly drawn from Azo's manuals of the Institutes and of the Code, a general analysis of actions. The very fact that an English justice should have felt the necessity of such a general introduction is extremely noteworthy.

Nor is his work in this line by any means a contemptible one. I do not propose to determine by exact marks what the school value of such work may be nowadays. But what we can do is to notice that Bracton's aim was as different from that of his model, the Bolognese doctor, as the means at his disposal were peculiar. He lived in a country which could not be compared with Italy in its standard of general culture, and especially in the wealth of classical tradition and scholarship. The Bolognese glossator provided a remarkable exegesis of the Institutes and of Justinian's Code ; he comments on his texts, illustrates and explains them, but does not remodel their doctrine—he speaks of *patria potestas*, of slavery, of the *Lex Aquilia*, of the interdicts, as if they were institutions which still obtained in the Italian practice of his time ; in doing this he does not consider modern practice, and he stands very near our own expositors of Roman Law: we might almost be induced to treat him as one of ourselves, as a citizen of our present republic of letters. Now such a standard would be entirely out of place in regard to Bracton. He does not want to state Justinian's teaching more or less exactly, but compiles Institutes for the English law of his time, and he attempts to build up these English Institutes with the help of Roman materials. There were no better materials at his disposal ; there was no body of doctrine which could show better the general notions with which legal thought must deal, and when we think of the place still occupied by the teaching of Roman Law in European schools, we shall not wonder at the course followed by Bracton. In fact, he attempted to do in a very systematic manner what his French contemporaries were doing in a much more casual fashion.

Some of the general principles expounded in the Institutes and in the commentaries to them might serve as an illuminating guide for English legal thought, while features entirely foreign to English life had to be removed. Thus the Introduction was undoubtedly intended to strengthen native legal doctrine by the infusion of legal conceptions of a high order drawn from the fountain head of civilised and scientific law. But there might also be a second aim, namely, to influence the material development of English legal doctrine, to provide it with clues for the solution of difficult problems, and to improve on the existing practice of the courts. Bracton aimed chiefly at the first of these results, although in some cases we may notice that he had in view to influence substantive law itself.

Let us turn, however, to Bracton's own work and take as examples some of its initial speculations.

3. On the very threshold he encounters an inevitable difficulty of his undertaking, and striking contrasts between English Law and Roman Law cause him to reflect on the great question as to the modes by which a legal rule is sanctioned and stated. Civil law as collected by Justinian and expounded by Azo was a definite body of doctrine sanctioned by Imperial authority,

and consigned to an authorised written version.
Now does English law afford a parallel in this
respect ? Where is the sanction of English Law
to be found ? How is one to recognise its rules ?
Both Glanvill and Bracton have been reflecting
on these questions. It is not absurd to give
English unwritten rules the designation of law,
because they proceed from a command of the
sovereign, the King, are established by the consent of the great men, and imply a promise of
obedience (*sponsio*) on the part of the commonwealth. Thus far Bracton, while Glanvill is not
only shorter but onesided—he deduces the authority of English law from the famous saying :
quod principi placuit legis habet vigorem—a
saying which was not in keeping with the political
tendencies of Simon de Montfort's time, and
therefore put aside by Bracton. In what sense
can it be said, however, that the consent of great
men is an element of English law ? At first
sight this may be true of Statutes and Assizes,
but hardly of the decisions of judges on which
the greater part of common law rests. But, as
Statutes and Assizes are written law, they do
not come within the scope of the argument at all.
It seems that the body of magnates, of great men
whose consent appears necessary for the making of
the law in England, is assumed to be identical with
the body of the Curia Regis, from which all jurisdiction proceeds. To its authority the sanction

of English legal rules is thus ultimately referred, although it remains always expressed in vague Romanesque terms.* We can see that a difficulty is felt as to the power of single judges to lay down the law, and it is settled in a way which reminds us of Beaumanoir. The Common law rules established by general custom ought to proceed from the whole court of the King, and their repeal and alteration is the affair of the whole court. In case of doubt recourse should be had to this court, which represents the *majores*, the magnates of the kingdom. Undoubtedly some of the great men, the judges and justiciars, one might be inclined to say, do not act up to this general doctrine, but lay down decisions as if their opinions were sufficient to constitute law. This is altogether reprehensible. The single judge is in the position of interpreter of the law, however, and though he is precluded from altering it at his wish, he may not only follow it when it is clear, but also improve upon it, an improvement not being an alteration. This reasoning is partly suggested by Azo's teaching as to the interpretation of law, and as to legal fictions by which the meaning of rules is widened, but it goes further both in wording and spirit, and though strained from a purely logical point of view, it very aptly opens a work which has to combine and contrast Civil law and English Common law.

* App. VIII.

ROMAN LAW IN ENGLAND

If the difficulty as to the authority and sanction of common law may be easily overcome, the second objection to the common form of English doctrine is recognised to be grounded on serious considerations. There is no authorised version of English legal rules. This is felt both by Glanvill and by Bracton. Very material drawbacks follow from the absence of such a version; law is perverted by the ignorance of beginners who ascend the bench before they have mastered the elements of legal lore; it is also perverted by the overbearing conceit of people in authority, who treat it according to their personal views and inclinations. It is to remedy these very drawbacks that both Glanvill and Bracton set out to perform their task, the first in a perfunctory and thoroughly practical manner, the other with a great store of authorities at his disposal. Bracton's work may be called a private treatise on the common law in its relation to general jurisprudence, and this literary departure remains significant for the further course of English legal studies.

4. There follow generalities about *justitia* and *jus*. The Bolognese doctor starts from the definition of justice as given in the Digest : " justice is a constant and permanent will to allow everyone his right " (*justitia est constans et perpetua voluntas jus suum cuique tribuendi*). According to scholastic method he takes up every word

in the sentence and expands it by interpretation so as to define the different attributes and conditions of justice. In this way he draws attention to the fact that justice may be considered as a divine institution, deciding once for all what is right and what is wrong. Or else it may be considered from the point of view of humanity. In this case the stress would lie on the will of man to do right, and not on external facts. Immutability and permanency are necessary attributes of justice. Variations or changes would destroy its very essence. If a legal privilege is first conceded and afterwards denied, this is in no way a change of justice, but a consequence of a change of acts. Bracton's summary of this section cuts short many of the philological distinctions. He finds himself confronted with a peculiarity of English phraseology, namely, with the absence of an equivalent in English to the word *jus*. Though writing in Latin, he does not want to make his teaching dependent on a foreign use of terms, and therefore he introduces, though very shortly, the terms *lex* and *consuetudo*—law and custom—explaining that they correspond to *jus*, which in this case would be rendered by the English word 'law.' But, we may add, the proper rendering of *jus* would not always be 'law,' the objective order of things and duties, as one might say, but sometimes 'right,' the subjective sphere, what I claim as my own against my neighbours. If Bracton had been making a translation, he would have found himself obliged to observe this variation of meaning. As it is, he uses Latin, although a Latin addressed to English readers, and this gives rise to what seems at first sight a gross blunder. Azo, talking of *jus* as 'law,' ridicules the idea that there could be the law of Peter or John, of a lion or of a donkey. Bracton, evidently speaking of *jus* as 'right,' turns the same sentence to positive account, and admits the right (*jus*) of Peter and of Paul. "The right of a lion or of a donkey" would, however, sound quaint enough, and it would have been better if Bracton had not gone so far on the subjective track. His meaning seems to have been, that we have to consider varieties of right derived from claims of divers beings and of claims in respect of divers things.

He differs from Azo yet another time when the contrast between *proprietas* (ownership) and *bonorum possessio* (possession) makes it necessary for him to notice a material difference in the use of these fundamental conceptions in Rome and in England. While the Roman lawyer draws a sharp distinction between ownership as the genuine and complete right to a thing, and possession as the protected enjoyment of it, the English lawyer merges both ideas in the intermediate and relative conception of seisin. A man is seised of a thing, more frequently of land,

and his seisin must be protected by the courts until a better ground of seisin has been found. B, the eldest son of A, may be his right heir, but if he did not obtain seisin on A's death, and C, the second son, has done so, C must be *prima facie* protected because he is already in seisin. He may be ousted only if B challenges his title and proves the truth of his contention. Bracton quite appropriately called attention to this fundamental difference of legal principle in a marginal note which eventually crept into the text itself, and destroyed the smooth course of Roman doctrine as set forth in Azo's manual.

There follows a section on the law of nature, the *jus civile* and the *jus gentium*. Azo, concerned with the interpretation of Roman texts as they stand, treats of the general philosophical problem of the law of nature as opposed to the positive law of States. But he also explains the purely Roman distinction between *jus civile* — the law of the Roman people — and the *jus gentium* — private law based on the legal customs of different nations. Bracton gives the substance of Azo's teaching on the law of nature, noticing the two possible meanings of the expression — as derived from the nature of live creatures, of animals as well as men, and as representing the rational concepts of man's nature. But he combines this second idea with that of the *jus gentium*, not taking much care to discover the historical differences between such reasonable rules and those imposed by the *jus civile*. In this respect he is undoubtedly inaccurate, but we can hardly reproach him, when we remember that even Roman jurists did not always distinguish clearly between the bidding of the *jus naturale* and the *ratio naturalis,* on which the rules of the *jus gentium* were supposed to be based. As for the *jus civile,* Bracton seeks to appropriate the expression in a way characteristic of mediæval usage. He has no interest in the original law of the Roman State, the *jus* of the Quirites, but there is one kind of law existing in England which might be designated by a reference to *jus civile.* This is the customary law of boroughs —*jus civitatum.*

5. The contrast between the professor expounding antiquarian doctrines, and the judge fitting English facts into a Roman frame, is especially striking in the treatment of the law of persons. Bracton follows Azo as to the principal and very important generalisation, " all men are either free or slaves." But such a generalisation had to be modified both in ancient Rome and in mediæval Italy or England. Azo proceeds to give the necessary commentary from the point of view of ancient Rome. He treats of *statu liberi* and of *adscripticii* to show that it is possible to arrange

these subordinate groups under the chief headings of free and unfree. He does not deal with the Italian world in which he lives, nor is he troubled by the fact that neither the *statu liberi* nor the *adscripticii* are known to his Bolognese or Florentine contemporaries. The English lawyer proceeds on an entirely different course. The *statu liberi* and *adscripticii* are used by him to illustrate actual English conditions, although they lose much of their antiquarian genuineness, thanks to this process of adaptation. Of the free (*liberi*) it is needless to speak at length, for they appear in England under the same name. Villains are equated with slaves — a far-reaching assumption. As the *adscripticii* represent a kind of intermediate stage between free and serf, their counterpart would be the *villain socmen* of ancient demesne, and, to some extent, the freemen holding in villainage. As for the *statu liberi*, Bracton employs this term to denote serfs enjoying a state of liberty, as for example, serfs dwelling as freemen on free soil. In this case they are *prima facie* protected by law, and any person claiming them as villains must bring an action (*de nativo habendo*), and assume the burden of proof in court. This is, of course, no Roman doctrine ; it is the adaptation of a Roman term to English distinctions.

At the end of the sections treating of the law

of persons Bracton returns to the problem of slavery, and lays stress on the fact that slaves are not completely in the power of their lords. He finds support for this contention in the later Roman doctrine which, through the influence of Stoicism and Christianity, granted some protection to the slave against exceptional cruelty on the part of the master. From the time of the Antonines, a master treating his slave in an intolerable manner, could be constrained by the magistrates to sell him. It was declared that the homicide of a slave by his master was a criminal offence. Azo took particular notice of these limitations of the power of masters over slaves, and adduced as a reason for the interference with the right of property in slaves, the importance for the Commonwealth of preventing owners from misusing their property (*expedit reipublicæ ne quis re sua male utatur*). Bracton not only endorses the doctrine, but adds an important concrete feature which shows that in this case he did not merely copy foreign learning, but was pleading for a certain point of view before English jurists. He defines the "intolerable injury" as a destruction by the master of the serf's waynage, that is, of his plough team which, as we know, was safe from Royal amercement. There are precedents for this view in Norman legal usage, forbidding the taking away of the rustic's waynage by the lord ; and, of course, in the fact that in Anglo-Saxon times the predecessor of the villain, the ceorl, was not a slave at all, but had a standing against his lord in the courts of law. But at the time when Bracton wrote, the defence of waynage did not tally with the surrender of the old rights of free cultivators in other respects. Bracton himself, representing the general drift of the jurisprudence of his time, had maintained that there was no difference between a serf and a villain. The reservations, he wished to draw in regard to the right of waynage, are akin to the vacillations of his brother judges in cases where there was at stake the right of men holding in villainage to appeal to the King's courts for remedies against their lords. After some contradictory decisions, the courts ended by applying strictly the rule that villains have no civil claims against their lords, and that, in law, what is held by the villain, is owned by the lord. At the same time the reservation as to waynage disappears. Bracton's teaching on villainage is thus very instructive, not merely from the point of view of the evolution of villain tenure, but also for estimating the practical influence of Romanesque learning on him and other English lawyers. Though the status of villains was undoubtedly developed chiefly by the pressure of economic and political forces, it is clear that the study of Roman precedents played an important part in the shaping of its legal rules. To put it in another way, the historical growth of English villainage did not necessarily involve its treatment on the basis of serfdom or slavery. But the infusion of Roman doctrine made the legal treatment of villainage harder than might have been the case otherwise, while the partial reservations introduced by the Emperors and admitted by Bracton did not carry much weight in practice.

Another case, where the study of Roman doctrine has left a distinct trace on English legal thought, is the well-known distinction between real and personal property. We may observe the actual origin of this famous distinction which still holds good at the present day. The root of it lies in the teaching of Roman lawyers on actions. There are real actions—*actiones in rem*—which aim at obtaining the property of a certain thing, and personal actions, urging certain claims against persons, requiring them to do something, to give something, or to forbear from something. The question of obtaining a specific object does not arise in the latter case. It is the value claimed that is of importance. So far, the teaching is common to both Roman and English lawyers. But Bracton and his fellow-judges, working on this basis, went a step beyond their Roman guides.

They used the distinction between actions to differentiate between different kinds of property. Land and interests connected with it appeared to them to be naturally the object of real actions, because here the claim was directed to a definite thing and to nothing else. On the other hand, chattels were, as a rule, claimed in the same way as rights, for example, as the performance of some labour or office. The aim of the action was to obtain either the thing or service, or its equivalent from the person under obligation. The distinction became fundamental in the English legal system. Again, a striking example of the influence of Roman distinctions is afforded by the treatment of leases for terms of years. Bracton and thirteenth century judges consider the lessees not as tenants having an estate of freehold, but as mere *usufructuarii*. This is altered to a great extent by later doctrine, but the initial classification has left its traces on the law of the subject.

Bracton and his compeers had especially much to learn from the Romans, and the glossators who expounded their doctrines, on the subject of obligations generated by contracts and torts. The exceedingly active economic intercourse of the Roman State in its most prosperous days had been utilised by keen jurists to frame a doctrine conspicuous, even in the domain of classical law, for its subtlety and dialectical resourcefulness. Part of this vast material had to be left on one side by Bracton, while other parts were adopted more for the sake of possible eventualities than for the immediate requirements of practice. Bracton appropriates the fundamental idea that a nude pact, a convention bereft of particular form, does not constitute an obligation enforceable at law. He cites a couple of doggerel lines intended as an assistance to the beginner in remembering what could serve as vestments to pacts. "*Re, verbis, scripto, consensu, traditione, junctura vestes sumere pacta solent.*"

The first three species apply to real contracts—such as, e.g., deposit ; to verbal contracts—the Roman solemn promise (*stipulatio*), or an equivalent of it in writing, the deed under seal, which came to be the principal mode of contracting in English law ; the fourth relates to consensual contracts—sale and hire by mutual consent, although in this respect English law could not be made to fit exactly the Roman view. Besides these Azo mentions two modes of clothing a bargain which he describes in quaint language. Whereas in the first four cases the contract is born vested, there are two occasions when it is bare at the moment of birth ; but once having seen the light, it begins to look about for suitable clothing, and, eventually, it may find furs which will protect it from frost and decay; this happens should delivery (*traditio*) supervene, or a condition which did not exist at the moment when the convention was made, but which, if it appears later on, renders it perfect and provides it with a vesture. All this is appropriated by Bracton in a slightly modified form, and this "reception" of the Roman doctrine provides a starting-point for subsequent development. First, the ecclesiastical courts and the Chancery, later on Common Law Courts, took part in the development of a doctrine concerning obligations which took account of informal agreements, and laid down rules as to their validity and enforcement.

On the whole it is clear that it is impossible to estimate the influence of Roman law in England by references to paragraphs of the Digest or of the Codex. If we want to find definite traces of it we have to look out not for references but for maxims, some of which, besides, had passed through the medium of Canon law.* The only real test of its character and extent is afforded by the development of juridical ideas, and in this respect the initial influence of Roman teaching on English doctrines will be found to be considerable. On many subjects the judges and legal writers of England were, as it were,

* E.g. *Year Books of Edw. II* (Selden Soc.), **I,** 5, 31, 186; **II,** 110, 176.

prompted by their Roman predecessors, and this intercourse of ideas is nowhere as conspicuous as in the frequent cases when English lawyers did not simply copy their Roman models, but borrowed suggestions from them in order to develop them in their own way.

LECTURE V

ROMAN LAW IN GERMANY

Authorities : *R. Schröder*, Deutsche Rechtsgeschichte, 1889; *H. Brunner*, Grundzüge der deutschen Rechtsgeschichte, 1887; *J. Bryce*, The Holy Roman Empire, 1904; *Jansen*, Geschichte des deutschen Volks, I, 1890; *Stintzing*, Geschichte der deutschen Rechtswissenschaft, 1880; Geschichte der populären Litteratur des römisch-kanonischen Rechts am Ende des Mittelalters, 1867; *Stintzing*, Ulrich Zasius, Die Juristen sind böse Christen, 1875; *Stobbe*, Geschichte der Rechtsquellen, 1860–64; *E. Seckel*, Beiträge zur Geschichte beider Rechte im Mittelalter, 1898; *Muther*, Zur Geschichte der Rechtswissenschaft und der Universitäten in Deutschland, 1876; *A. Stölzel*, Die Entwickelung des gelehrten Richterthums, 1872; *G. v. Below*, Die Ursachen der Rezeption des römischen Rechts in Deutschland, 1905; *Modderman*, Die Reception des römischen Rechts, übersetzt von K. Schurz, 1875; *C. A. Schmidt*, Die Rezeption des römischen Rechts in Deutschland, 1868; *O. Gierke*, Deutsches Genossenschaftsrecht, 1873; *J. Kohler*, Beiträge zur Geschichte des römischen Rechts in Deutschland, 1896; *Landsberg*, Ueber die Entstehung der Regel, "Quidquid non agnoscit glossa, non agnoscit forum," 1890.

1. THE influence of Roman Law on Germany is marked by very peculiar conditions. It seemed at the outset as if there would not be much room for Roman doctrine in a country with a German-speaking population of Germanic stock. But yet at a later period, some time in the fifteenth century, the legal

life of Germany was forced into an entirely new channel by the wholesale "reception" of Roman Law. To give a clear idea of the circumstances which brought about this startling result, I must first say a few words on the political and legal conditions of Germany at the close of the Middle Ages.

The downfall of the Swabian dynasty and the painful Interregnum in the third quarter of the thirteenth century revealed the unsound basis of the magnificent structure of the Holy Roman Empire. While stretching over Italy and Burgundy, it had failed to strike firm roots in native German soil, and it fell to pieces in spite of the brilliant achievements of some of its rulers. The Hapsburg and Luxemburg princes, who succeeded to the Imperial crown after the Interregnum, were chiefly interested in constructing the fabric of their household—in uniting various principalities to form a patrimony for their families, and in strengthening their princely power in these territories. The German Empire, as such, the "Reich," became more than ever a loose confederation of numberless political units without effective central government ; it could not even prevent feuds among its members—the various dukes, counts, barons, abbots, and towns. The Emperor Frederick III, whose reign occupied a whole half of the fifteenth century, did not set foot on Imperial ground for twenty-five years (1444–71). The surrender of sovereign authority to the princes was formally recognised in respect of the more important ones, the seven electors (Kurfürsten), by the Golden Bull, but in practice, the measure of political importance enjoyed by all the different "estates" of the realm (Stände) depended merely on strength and opportunity. The central court of the Empire, the "Reichshofgericht," was hardly more than a name. When a case came up to it for decision, assessors had to be collected for the special purpose, litigation was interminable, while the means for executing the sentence were quite inadequate. It is not to be wondered at that the various representatives of political authority in the country relied much more on alliances and leagues than on Imperial justice, or on the decrees of the Imperial Diet (Reichstag). The towns formed powerful confederations, and they were met by still more powerful leagues of princes. After the two great struggles of 1388 and of 1450 and countless smaller feuds, a certain order was guaranteed by regional leagues, like the Swabian or the Rhenish, including both princes and towns, for the purpose of maintaining a more or less precarious peace.

It is clear that the legal arrangements of a society living under such political conditions were necessarily peculiar. Jurisdiction and law were, as it were, pulverised into a quantity of smaller and larger fractions. Each principality, lordship, town, followed a law of its own. And apart from the disruption of these circles of territorial customs, numberless variations were produced by the social status of the parties concerned — the law of knights and of fees (Lehnrecht) was differentiated not only from the law of the country in general (Landrecht), but also from manorial law (Hofrecht), municipal law (Stadtrecht), guild law (Zunftrecht), peasant law (Bauernrecht). Besides, there was the great cleavage between lay and ecclesiastical courts. The fundamental principle of German law amounted to a recognition of the right of each group of citizens to apply their own customary ideas in the dealings of their members with each other. This is an excellent principle, productive of freedom and of exuberant development, but it stands clearly in need of strong set-off in the way of co-ordination between the centrifugal forces of all those local groups. And the centripetal tendency, so necessary in such a case, was sadly wanting. The political disruption of the Empire made it impossible to reduce local customs to one common law by the power of the State and of its tribunals. German law as a unity did not exist at the close of the Middle Ages. It was broken up into countless local customs, which, for this very reason, were unable to tackle the wider problems of civil intercourse.

A second difficulty sprang from the composition of the various tribunals and from the manner in which law was laid down in them. Statutory law formed naturally a rare exception. There were some enactments passed by the Diets, chiefly concerning questions of public law, and occasional statutes passed in the different principalities and towns. But most legal questions had to be settled finally by un-written and unenacted law, which had to be ascertained or " found " for the purpose. German tribunals of all degrees had standing organs for the finding of law—the Schöffen or assessors. The judge (Richter) presided over the court, directed its proceedings and put questions to the assessors. It was the duty of the latter to give decisions or sentences (Urtheil) on all points of law raised by the presiding magistrate. As for questions of fact, they were settled by formal methods of inquiry—by battle, oath, witnesses, and the production of deeds. Thus everything hinged on the "find-ing " of the law by the Schöffen, representing the legal opinions of a certain social or political group. Now these Schöffen, though not im-panelled for a few days like modern jurors, but serving in the courts as standing assessors, were nevertheless laymen. What they knew of law was gathered chiefly from personal experience and occasional information, or suggested by practical wisdom. The laws of the different groups thus remained in close touch with popular conceptions and sometimes rose to a considerable excellence in their treatment of legal problems, but they were not connected with any scientific system and lacked precision. And yet, at a certain stage of economic and social development, law stands in need of school learning and technical skill. Thus it came to pass that, at the very moment when German social arrangements were progressing from mediæval to modern conditions, when its town life was enjoying a kind of hothouse prosperity resulting from its commerical relations with Italy and the Levant on the one side, Flanders, the Scandinavian North, Poland, and Russia on the other, German law was crippled by · particularistic tendencies and by a lack of professional learning. Further progress could only be achieved by the creation of a Common Law based on systematised knowledge.

2. It is interesting to watch the attempts to get rid of the obvious drawbacks of German law by means of institutions of native origin. One expedient, which obtained considerable success in municipal jurisdiction, was the reference of doubtful cases from local to superior courts. These superior courts (Oberhöfe) were

constituted in some of the more important cities with which other towns were closely allied, either as colonies or as members of the same league. Such were the Oberhöfe of Frankfort-on-the-Main for the Rhine provinces, of Lübeck for the Hanseatic towns, of Magdeburg for Saxony, Thuringia and the German settlements in the East. The practice of the Oberhöfe naturally helped to systematise to some extent the varieties that had grown up in private law.

Another powerful influence in the same direction was exercised by the spread of authoritative treatises on customary law. The most remarkable and influential of these was compiled by Eike von Repgow on the law of the Saxons (Sachsenspiegel). It may be compared with Bracton's famous work on the laws of England, with this characteristic difference, that the English author wrote on the common. law of his country, while the German treated of the legal customs of one German race. But, in spite of this material limitation, Eike von Repgow's work was an historical achievement. It provided the courts of Saxon Germany with a firm basis of jurisprudence, which was widely accepted and maintained. A most striking effect of this authoritative statement is revealed by the fact that the Northern territories, armed with the jurisprudence of the Sachsenspiegel, opposed a stubborn resistance to the inroads of Roman Law. This proves that the wholesale "reception" of Roman rules is not accounted for by any inherent incompetence in German law. Where, as in Saxon lands, excessive particularism and uncertainty were counteracted, German law proved quite able to stand its ground.

Other statements of provincial custom testify to the rising tide of Roman ideas. The *German Mirror* appeals in a general way to the guidance of the masters of law, that is, of the Roman jurists, and the *Swabian Mirror* shows distinct borrowings from Roman legal sources. Johann von Buch, the author of a gloss to the *Saxon Mirror*, composed some time between 1325 and 1355, finds it necessary to corroborate the rules of the *Saxon Mirror* by instituting comparisons with similar Roman rules; and at the same time a town clerk, Johann of Brünn, was engaged in the compilation of a regular textbook of Roman Law for German practitioners.

These are sure indications that Roman Law was beginning to assert itself as a remedy for the shortcomings of German jurisprudence. To explain this phenomenon we must take into account, to begin with, that in the view of educated Germans, the Holy Roman Empire had united Germany and Rome; the Emperors of the German race were deemed the direct successors of Constantine and Justinian. Frederick Barbarossa and Frederick II appealed to their hereditary right as successors of the Roman emperors of old, and actually inserted some of their own enactments as a sequel to the Novellæ of Justinian. Mediæval people had no strong sense of historical diversities. Artists of the period did not scruple to represent the guests at the wedding in Cana in doublets and slouched hats. Nor was there anything incongruous in the idea that the *Corpus Juris Civilis* was the Imperial law of Sigismund or Frederick III as rulers of the Holy Roman Empire. The Church, the other cosmopolitan power of the time, helped to propagate a similar theory. It had worked out a Canon law of its own, and had come to draw definite boundaries between the decrees of that law and the *leges* of secular authorities. But the jurisprudential affinity of both Codes, the ecclesiastical and the civil, was obvious, and at the universities the studies of both were necessarily allied. It came to be so at Prague and in the purely German universities that followed it—Erfurt, Cologne, Rostock, Heidelberg, Leipzig, Greifswald, etc. It is true that the principal chairs in the law faculties of these universities were chairs of Canon law, but the holders of them were frequently doctors of both laws (*utriusque juris*), lecturing in Civil as well as in Canon law. In Prague and in

Rostock the former branch of study was already regarded as a necessary part of the systematic *curriculum*. At first many of the law professors were Italians, but gradually Germans came forward, and although no first-rate scholar can be named among them before Ulrich Zasius, professor at Freiburg, and Schürpf at Wittenberg (about 1500), yet the large number of teachers and pupils proves the increasing practical importance of the study.

3. Even more weighty evidence is forthcoming from the text-books of Roman and Canon law, produced in the fourteenth and especially in the fifteenth century. These books were intended to assist persons who had not sufficient time to spend on a thorough and prolonged study of legal sources, but who, at the same time, desired to make use of the accumulated wisdom of Roman jurisprudence. Such was, for example, the *Vocabulary* of both laws of Jodocus, a work composed by an Erfurt doctor about 1452 and extensively circulated in Germany and other countries. Fifty-two editions of it were issued during the fifty years between 1473 and 1523. The *Vocabulary* gives short definitions and explanations of all sorts of terms used by Roman jurisconsults and enactments. [It is sufficiently clear and well-informed.

A curious expression of this striving towards

the acquisition of Roman legal ideas and forms
may be found in a widely diffused branch of the
juridical literature of the time, namely, the
so-called "trials of Satan." It was a favourite
concept of theologians to expound the doctrine of salvation by using the form of a fictitious
trial. The object was to show that by the
Saviour's sacrifice, hell had lost its power over
mankind, and that the atonement, consequent
on this sacrifice, could be claimed as a matter,
not only of grace, but of justice. One of these
tracts was ascribed, and probably rightly, to no
less a jurist than the Bolognese Doctor, Bartolus,
and a German translation, named after Belial,
lays stress on the excellent information it
supplies on questions of procedure. The substance of the latter discourse is as follows.
Satan appears before the tribunal of Christ
under the name of Mascaron, and presents a
complaint against mankind. Christ assigns a
hearing. The defendant failing to put in an
appearance on the assigned day, the plaintiff
claims judgment by default, but Christ declares
that He grants an adjournment on the ground
of equity and on the strength of His discretionary
powers as judge. The next day the Virgin
Mary appears as an advocate for mankind.
Mascaron objects to her being admitted to
represent the defendant, firstly, because she is
a woman and therefore unfit to be an advocate,

and secondly, on account of her relationship to the judge. Christ overrides the objection and the case proceeds. The action brought by Mascaron is an *actio spolii*, an action for despoiling hell of its possession. The Virgin demurs, on the ground that hell was only entitled to the Detinue of mankind, and was bound to safe-keeping in the interest of God. The *actio spolii* is not allowed by the court. Satan tries then to bring a petitory action ; he demands a sentence against mankind on the ground of original sin and of the words of God : on "the day when thou eatest of the fruit of the tree, thou shalt die." The Virgin excepts against this : hell itself was the cause of the Fall and is not entitled to reap the benefit of its own fraud (*dolus*). Satan comes with a replication : even were this right, mankind ought to be condemned *officio judicis,* by the action of the court, because justice ought not to leave crime unpunished. The Virgin protests against such a new departure as an illegal alteration of the count. Besides, there is a decisive argument for the defendant, namely, that Christ has suffered punishment for mankind, and satisfied justice by His voluntary sacrifice. Mascaron is therefore dismissed by the court.

It may be observed that all sorts of points on procedure are introduced in this example, evidently with the idea of acquainting beginners with technical terms and fundamental forms of pleading, such as summons, default, equity, possessory and petitory action, exception, replication, count, fraud, etc.

A popular work of another kind is the *Mirror of Actions,* a production dating from the beginning of the fifteenth century. The author, probably some town clerk, wrote his book in the frontier district between Swabia and Franconia, perhaps in the little town of Schwäbisch Hall. He is deeply grieved at the uncertainty of German legal customs, the greed and violence of princes, the slackness of the Emperor. He wants his fatherland to build up its laws on the basis of the Roman code, without neglecting ancient and reasonable customs. His first book, dedicated to private law, is partly derived from a work of Roffredus, a Bolognese doctor, and partly from the more elementary treatise of John de Blanosco (de actionibus, 1259). The German author endeavours, for the most part, to give a plain and useful statement of Roman rules, and avoids pedantic subtleties. It is not easy, of course, to combine German legal principles with the learned apparatus and the peculiar distinctions of Roman jurists, and it cannot be said that our author has succeeded in producing a thoroughly logical and clear amalgamation of both bodies of law. Yet his attempt is of the utmost importance, in that it shows that the introduction of such technical machinery as the Roman scheme of actions was, as early as the fifteenth century, not merely a subject for book learning, but directly affected practitioners. We find the *Mirror of Actions* (*Klagspiegel*) trying to fit German class distinctions into the social classification of Rome in the same manner as this was done by Bracton. It translates fluently the Latin *servus* by *Eigen Mann*, that is, by 'serf.' The equivalent in modern German would be *Leibeigen*, a man whose body is owned by another. Sometimes, however, the author is startled by the incongruity of such an identification, and is careful to add that slavery or even serfdom does not exist in German law. But then in the country, if not in the towns, there were numerous rustics who might appropriately be termed serfs (*leibeigen*), and therefore the *Klagspiegel* "receives," copies, many of the rules originally laid down for Roman slaves. In the same way there is a good deal of Romanesque learning in the treatment of obligations. Yet the author of the *Klagspiegel* does not seem to notice the difficulties felt by Roman lawyers in regard to the enforcement of 'nude' promises. He admits that they should be made the subject of actions. Again, his treatment of *emphyteusis*, of the hereditary lease of Roman Law, is strongly coloured by the fact that he uses the peasant tenancies of German mediæval custom as concrete material for his scheme.

119

Rents and services become the chief feature in the relation between the lord and his tenant (*Hintersasse*) ; the rights of the lord to supervise the cultivation, and to exercise a disciplinary power over the tenant, are recognised as an ancient incident of the tenure, etc. As a commentary on Roman sources, all this is erroneous, but in the history of "reception" this and similar variations from the orthodox doctrine are interesting and significant. They prove that we are confronted with something different from mere literary borrowings ; we witness the struggle between Roman and German theories in practice.

4. The next point to be observed concerns the influence of the knowledge of Roman Law acquired in the Universities and through popular or learned treatises on practice. We can easily discern that the persons who had recourse to Roman texts and to Romanistic literature in the fifteenth century belonged for the most part to one or other of three classes. There were, firstly, ecclesiastics desirous of confirming their contentions on church matters and private matters by reference to Civil law, to which Canon law was closely allied ; secondly, town clerks acting as jurisconsults to cities and to princes, and taking part in the discussions of ordinary tribunals as assessors ; thirdly, barristers in search of arguments for their clients ; they displayed a natural bent towards the written Common

law of Rome, in preference to the native wisdom of German assessors (the Schöffen). But through what channels was Roman Law introduced into courts of law or into administrative offices ?

Juridical consultation formed the principal medium for its application in the earlier stages of the process. Officials in doubt as to some intricate problem of private or administrative law, and also parties to complicated suits, began to seek the advice of well-known jurists, especially of doctors of laws at the Universities. An early example is presented by the action of the Council of Cologne at the close of the fourteenth century in connection with the so-called Brotherhoods of Common Life (Brüder des gemeinsamen Lebens) —associations of fervently religious persons of both sexes, who joined in a common life of work and prayer. Consultations have been preserved on the question as to whether such associations were to be allowed or not, whether they were *collegia licita*, according to Roman terminology, or not. The first of these consultations is signed by two doctors and two licentiates of laws of the University of Cologne, of whom the two first were holders of regular chairs of law (*legum doctores actu regentes in legibus*). The case is put in the following manner :

" In certain places persons join to live in common. Some are ecclesiastics dwelling in one house, where they are engaged in writing lawful books. Others, who cannot write, are engaged in mechanical crafts in another house. Or else they do manual work. These persons living in the two houses work and live on the results of their labour, and divide among themselves the proceeds and their own goods, should they have any. They take their meals together, and do not beg for alms, and they have a rector who takes charge of the hall. They obey him as good disciples obey their master, and they settle the hours for work and the hours for rest, and similar matters. They choose to enjoy their goods in common, that they may live more quietly. The principal object in such a life is not to make profit, but they hope that by so living they may please God and serve Him. Such is the theme. It is asked whether such a college is an allowed one, and whether they have a right to elect a rector, to make by-laws for themselves, and to do other things allowed to colleges. And also what is the law in regard to women who live apart from their husbands, and sew and spin and exercise textile crafts on which they live in the same way (as described above)?" The doctors of Civil law gave an entirely favourable opinion on the authority of Bartolus, with the adjunct that women could only join in such a college provided their work was not repugnant to womanhood (*si statui muliebri non repugnet*). The consultation of the canonists based on Jo-

hannes Andreæ was to the effect that no attempt
to start new religious beliefs was permissible,
but that life in a society was not illicit in itself.
I may add that the brothers of Common Life
had to endure many attacks from jealous Church-
men, but the Council of Constance supported
them, and their communities and schools continued to flourish throughout the fifteenth century. In any case, the above-mentioned consultation is interesting from two points of view ;
its subject is the momentous apostolic revival
of Gerhard de Groot and his lay brotherhood ;
it also marked a step in the introduction of the
Roman theory of corporations into Germany.
The ruling both of the legists and of the canonists
is based on the Roman conception of the *universitas*
as a juridical person, of the creation of a fictitious
moral being endowed with the same rights as an
individual, and organised in such a way as to
ensure action for certain allowable aims in a
continuous manner. A rector and obligatory
by-laws are necessary to ensure such action ;
civil rights are ascribed to the society in question
on the pattern of other lawful societies ; the
individuality of its members is merged in certain
respects in the higher being of the corporation ;
the only point admitting of doubt concerns the
allowable aim of the latter. Once this is established
everything else follows of itself from the Roman
theory of the juridical person. We are able to

understand now why a consultation was needed, and what it supplied from the legal point of view to the authorities in Cologne. The Germanistic point of view as to corporations was a different one—it amounted to the admission of joint action by a plurality (Gesammtheit) acting as a union (Genossenschaft). This conception had not, however, reached a stage of theoretical completeness and of a conscious co-ordination of all details under the ruling principle. The Roman doctrine supplied this very requirement, and it was substituted as being more scientific and thorough.

Another characteristic set of consultations given by the Cologne jurists in the course of the fourteenth and the fifteenth centuries concerns difficulties arising from the adjustment of political and private rights in cities and principalities. The formation within the precincts of the Empire of commonwealths of different types created by express delegation, by force, by custom, and by prescription, gave rise to constant disputes and complications both in Italy and in Germany. One of the great Italian jurists of the fourteenth century, Bartolus, had instituted a new treatment of this troublesome department of municipal law. He adapted and developed Roman conceptions of the authority of the people as a source of power, of the part played by coercion in the creation of law (*vis coactiva*), of the delegation

of political authority and jurisdiction by the
Emperor, and the like. His commentaries on
the subject became the basis of the public law
of central Europe, and it is significant that the
professors of Roman Law in Germany appropriated
his doctrine in preference to the teaching of
Justinian's Code itself. The modern elements
of Bartolus' teaching made it the more acceptable
for the solution of problems arising out of the
tangled web of affairs in fifteenth-century Germany. It is in its Italian garb that Roman Law
was received by the Germans, and this modification explains to a great extent the reason of
the comparative ease of its adoption.

It is needless to add that in a state of government and society as that which prevailed in
Germany in the fifteenth century, the cross
relations between different political units and
social groups were constantly producing friction
and juridical disputes. And in all such questions,
German legal arrangements, based primarily on
local customs, failed signally. Recourse to
Roman Law as " Common law " was natural and
unavoidable. It assumed the form of awards
as well as of consultations. It became more and
more usual for parties to a suit to submit the
points in dispute to the arbitration of doctors of
law. One characteristic method of submitting
cases for decision to learned lawyers was the
institution of the so-called " Actenversendung,"

the transmission of the documents relating to a case by the court which had jurisdiction, to the law faculty of a famous university. The professors of the faculty acting *in corpore* considered the evidence and pleadings, sometimes demanding supplementary material, and ultimately formulated a decision. This was forwarded to the court. Needless to add, that this " transmission of acts " could only take place in connection with a procedure based on written documents. The rules of such a procedure followed the practice of ecclesiastical courts, and were largely derived from usages of later Roman Law. Thus the "Actenversendung," apart from the fact that it was an appeal to colleges of jurists trained in foreign law, furthered the process of Romanisation by the procedure necessary to effect it.

5. I have dwelt more particularly on the beginnings of " reception " in the fifteenth century, because the motives and reasons of the process are, as usual, more clearly apparent in their origins than in later developments. But the practical side of the process, the harvest of results in jurisdiction and legislation, belongs chiefly to the sixteenth century. The German courts of law, with their peculiar procedure and customary lore were overwhelmed by tribunals following Roman doctrine, primarily in consequence of the organisation of a central Imperial court, the " Reichskammergericht." This court deliber-

ately adopted Roman Law for its guidance as
the common law of the Empire. This occurred
in 1495, when the "Reichskammergericht" was
definitely constituted as a standing tribunal.
The event took place in connection with a movement towards the strengthening of Imperial
institutions in the reign of Maximilian I. The
Empire was reformed as a federation for maintaining public peace, divided into regions and
circles, and subordinated in a legal sense to the
"Reichskammergericht." This High Court never
attained, of course, the decisive influence of the
English Royal courts, or of French Parlements,
but, nevertheless, it provided a point of concentration for the Common law of the Empire;
and, in spite of its dilatoriness and weakness in
execution, it exercised a considerable influence
on the juridical institutions of all the estates of
the Empire. At the outset, it was enacted that
half of its sixteen assessors should be doctors of
laws, the other half being knights. Later on,
it was decreed that even the knights should, so
far as possible, be chosen from among persons
learned in the Civil law. A tribunal thus constituted threw all its weight into the scale of
the "reception" of foreign law against native
customary jurisprudence. The law of Justinian
was received *in complexu*, in its details and in its
entirety, with the characteristic limitation, however, that it was adopted not directly from the

original sources, but from the texts as glossed by Italian scholars. The rule that doctrines not recognised by the glossators are not to be taken into consideration by the judges (*quod non agnoscit glossa non agnoscit forum*), was more than a confession of literary subordination to the greater knowledge of Azo, Accursius, Bartolus, Baldus, etc. It was necessary in order to avoid details too intimately connected with ancient life, and entirely unsuited for importation.

The example set by the " Reichskammergericht " was immediately followed by the High Courts of the various principalities, and "reception " spread from the top to the bottom of the ladder. The importance of this gradual assimilation by the lower courts, of the leading principles of the superior tribunals, is well illustrated, for example, in the history of "reception " in the principalities of Julich and Berg (in the Rhine province). The estates of these principalities resolved in 1534 and 1537 to remodel their laws on Roman patterns, in order to avoid clashing with the superior court of the " Reichskammergericht." Under the influence of such various considerations, a movement towards the codification of local laws on the basis of their reformation and of the reception of Roman doctrine, sweeps over Germany. The towns of Worms and Nürenberg (A.D. 1479) are among the first to carry through such reformations. Most of the monarchically organised principalities follow suit, with the notable exception of some of the North German states, which remained faithful to a jurisprudence based on the "Sachsenspiegel."

The "reception" appears in this light mainly as a movement of the upper classes and of the political authorities connected with them. It encountered a good deal of opposition in the lower orders. Jurists were regarded as bad Christians (*Die Juristen sind böse Christen*). Every now and then one or the other among them was exposed to contumelious treatment, as, for example, two Constance doctors, whom a court of Schöffen in Thurgau put to flight, because it did not want to hear about Bartele and Baldele (Bartolus and Baldus), and was resolved to uphold its ancient customs. The revolutionary peasantry in 1525 declared in a fictitious document, nicknamed "The Reformation of the Emperor Frederick III," "that all doctors of laws should be abolished, and that justice should be administered according to the law of Moses, because it is not good for men to get better law than that proclaimed by God." Ulrich von Hutten was never tired of inveighing against the greedy, ignorant, pedantic set of lawyers, who spread darkness over the simplest questions, and use their pretentious learning to fleece the poor public. But, on the whole, the "reception" of foreign Common law was affected with much less strife and opposition than might have been expected from the radical nature of the experiment. The learned judges of Germany became judges in Civil law. The fundamental incongruity of the attempt was only realised much later, when native legal customs were resuscitated from oblivion and contemptuous relegation to the lowest local courts. The revenge of German law against artificial reception was achieved in our days by men like Heusler, Beseler, Gierke. And the weapons they wielded were forged from the general doctrines of German law, reconstructed by the help of its history.

Is it allowable to draw a moral from a complex historical process like the one we have been examining ? It seems as if, in spite of all varieties of tone and mood, two or three leading strains were constantly recurring in its course. It is evident, to begin with, that the reception of Roman Law depended largely on *political* causes ; this legal system was subordinated to the idea of the State towering over individuals or classes, and free from the intermixture of private and public interests characteristic of feudalism. It was bound to appeal to the minds of all the pioneers of the State conception—to ambitious Emperors, grasping territorial princes, reforming legists, and even clerical representatives of law and order. Coming, as it did, from an age of highly developed social intercourse, Roman Law satisfied in many respects the requirements of *economic* development. Although history never repeats itself, and the conditions of industry and trade in fourteenth-century Europe differed widely from those prevailing in the Roman Empire, the results of a vast experience in setting legal frames to business dealings had been accumulated in the Roman lawbooks, and the progressive classes of the closing Middle Ages did not fail to utilise them. This influence is especially manifest in the law of contracts. Lastly, from the *jurisprudential* point of view the scientific value of Roman Law could not be contested; it asserted itself as soon as there reappeared theoretical reflection on legal subjects. And when the elaboration of Common law became a social necessity, the Roman system grew to be a force not only in the schools, but also in the courts. Altogether, the history of Roman Law during the Middle Ages testifies to the latent vigour and organising power of *ideas* in the midst of shifting surroundings.

APPENDIX

I. (to p. 13).

Lex Romana Curiensis, IV.

De responsis prudentum.

Codex Theodosianus, 1, 4, 3.
Impp. Theodosius et Va-
lentinianus A A ad Sena-
tum urbis Romæ. Inter-
pretatio. Hæc lex osten-
dit, quorum iuris condito-
rum sententiæ valeant, hoc
est Papiniani Pauli, Gaii,
Ulpiani, Modestini, Scæ-
volæ, Sabini, Iuliani atque
Marcelli, quorum si fuerint,
prolatæ diversæ sententiæ,
ubi maior numerus unum
senserit, vincat. Quod si
forsitan æqualis numerus in
utraque parte sit, eius par-
tis præcedat auctoritas, in
qua Papinianus cum æquali
numero senserit, quia ut
singulos Papinianus vincit,
ita et cedit duobus. Scæ-
vola, Sabinus, Iulianus atque Marcellus in suis cor-
poribus non inveniuntur,
sed in præfatorum opere
tenentur inserti.

Imp. Theodosius. In-
terpretatio. Hæc causa
sicut Papiani, Pauli, Gagii,
Ulpiani, Modestini et Scifola, Savini, Iuliani atque
Marcelli est. Isti viri clar-
issimi consilium in suis cor-
poribus melius esse non
cognoverint, et in his libris
sic continent. Ubi de ac-
cionem indiciarie contendi-
tur, vel ubi inter duos
heredes de ipsorum facul-
tatem intencione inter se
habuerint, si unus de illis
habuerit amplius homines,
qui eius causam teneant,
quam ille alius : qui mai-
orem numerum habuerit de
bonos homines, ipse in iu-
dicio secundum legem suam
causam vincat. Et si for-
sitan de homines equalem
numerum habuerint, prece-
dat eius auctoritas, qui in
lege Papiani pro se alicum
titulum invenerit, ipsa causa vincat.

APPENDIX

II. Liutprand 134 (to p. 23).

Si hominis in uno vico habitantis aliqua intentionis habuerit de campo aut vinea prado aut silva vel de alias res, et collexerent se una pars cum virtutem et dixerent " quia wifamus et expellimus eum de ipsum locum per virtutem foras," et ambolaverunt, et scandalum ibi commissum fuerit et plagas aut feritas factas vel homo occisus fuerit : ita decernimus, ut plagas et feritas aut hominem mortuum conponant secundum anteriorem edicto, quod gloriosus Rothari rex vel nos instituimus ; pro autem inlecita presumptionem de ipsa collectionem conponat solidos 20 ad illam partem, qui in campum aut in vitis vel in prado aut in silva suum laborem faciebat. Hoc autem ideo statuimus, ut nullus presumat malas causas in qualiscumque locum excitare aut facere et non potuimus causam istam adsimilare, neque ad arischild, neque ad consilium rusticanorum, neque ad rusticanorum seditione : et plus congruum nobis paruit esse de consilium malum, id est de consilio mortis. Quia quando se collegunt et super alius vadunt pro peccatis, ad id ipsum vadunt ut malum faciant, aut si casus evenerit, hominem occidant, et plagas aut feritas faciant : ideo, ut dixemus, adsimilavimus causam istam ad consilium mortis, quod sunt, sicut supra premisimus, solidi vigenti.

III. Origines, V, c. 24, § 25 (to p. 28).
De instrumentis legalibus.

Donatio est cuiuslibet rei transactio. Dictam autem dicunt donationem quasi doni actionem, et dotem quasi do item. Præcedente enim in nuptiis donatione dos sequitur.

Conditio quid est (V, c. 24, § 29).

Conditio a condicendo quasi condiciones quia non ibi testis unus jurat, sed duo vel plures ; non enim in unius ore sed in duorum aut trium stat omne verbum. Item condictiones dicuntur quod inter se conveniat sermo testium quasi condictiones.

IV. *Glossa Irnerii* (to p. 55).

" Cum equitas et jus in hisdem rebus versentur, differunt tamen. Equitatis enim proprium est id quod justum est simpliciter proponere. Juris autem idem proponere volendo, scilicet aliquantum auctoritate subnecti. Quod propter hominum lapsus multum ab ea distare contingit, partim minus quam equitas dictaverit continendo, partim plus quam oporteat proponendo. Multis quoque aliis modis equitas et jus inter se differunt, cujus dissensus interpretatio, ut lex fiat, solis principibus destinatur" (quoted by Meynial, *Encore Irnerius*, N. R. L. de dr. fr., 1897, p. 352).

V. Glossæ Vacarii ad D.I. 3 (to p. 56).

(From the MS. of the Dean and Chapter of Worcester.)

1. Conditor autem et interpres legum solus est imperator. Scilicet ex propria volumtate. Ceteri ex necessitate. Item iudicis interpretatio nulla intelligitur preterquam si nullo ab his inter quos iudicat iuris remedio infirmetur, inter eos tantum tenet.

2. Generale et naturale congruum ut eo modo solvatur quid quo constructum est. Imperatoris autem constitutionem inuito populo immo et reclamante interdum fieri contingit et valet. Ergo et durat ut nec per consuetudinem abrogari possit nisi prius imperium et potestatem a principe amotam populus recipiat.

VI. (to p. 69).

Dig. I, 3, 32 pr. (Julianus). De quibus causis scriptis legibus non utimur, id custodire oportet quod moribus et consuetudine inductum est :

Beaumanoir, Prologue : Nous entendons a confermer grant partie de cest livre par les jugemens qui ont esté fet en nos tans en ladite contée de Clermont ; et l'autre partie par clers usages et par cleres coustumes usees et acoustumees de lonc tans pesiblement ;

et si qua in re hoc deficeret, tunc quod proximum et consequens ei est :

si nec id quidem appareat, tunc jus, quo urbs Roma utitur, servari oportet.

et l'autre partie, des cas douteus en ladite contée, par le jugement des chasteleries voisines ;

et l'autre partie par le droit qui est communs a tous on roiaume.

VII. Coutume de Beauvaisis, 31 (to p. 82).

Pour ce que mout seroit longue chose et chargeant as hommes qui font les jugemens de metre en jugement tous les cas qui vienent devant le baillif, li baillis doit metre grant peine de delivrer ce qui est pledié devant lui, quant il set que l'en doit fere du cas selonc la coustume et quant il voit que la chose est clere et aperte. Mes ce qui est en doute et les grosses quereles doivent bien estre mises en jugement ; ne il ne convient pas que l'on mete en jugement le cas qui a autre fois esté jugiés, tout soit ce que li jugemens soit fes pour autres persones, car l'on ne doit pas fere divers jugemens d'un meisme cas.

VIII. (Bracton I, 1 § 2, 1 § 3) (to p. 92).

Cum autem fere in omnibus regionibus utatur legibus et iure scripto, sola Anglia usa est in suis finibus jure non scripto et consuetudine, in ea quidem ex non scripto ius venit quod usus comprobavit, sed non erit absurdum leges Anglicanas, licet non scriptas, leges apellare, cum legis vigorem habeat quicquid de consilio et consensu magnatum et reipublicæ communi sponsione, auctoritate regis sive principis præcedente, iuste fuerit definitum et approbatum. Sunt etiam in Anglia consuetudines plures et diversæ secundum diversitatem locorum. habent enim Anglici plura ex consuetudine quæ non habent ex lege, sicut in diversis comitatibus, civitatibus, burgis et villis, ubi semper inquirendum erit quæ sit illius loci consuetudo et qualiter utantur consuetudine qui consuetudines allegant.

Cum autem huiusmodi leges et consuetudines per

insipientes et minus doctos, qui cathedram iudicandi ascendunt antequam leges didicerint, sæpius trahantur ad abusum, et qui stant in dubiis et in opinionibus, et multotiens pervertantur a maioribus, qui potius proprio arbitrio quam legum auctoritate causas decidunt, ad instructionem saltem minorum, ego Henricus de Brattone ' animum erexi ' ad vetera indicia iustorum, perscrutando diligenter, non sine vigiliis et labore, facta ipsorum, consilia et responsa, et quicquid inde nota dignum inveni in unam summam redigendo.

WILLIAM BRENDON AND SON, LTD.
PRINTERS, PLYMOUTH